LEAD GUITAR WORKSHOP

Lead Guitar: MODES

L.&.W
LEAD GUITAR WORKSHOP

Library of Congress Control Number:

Any references to historical events, real people, or real places are used fictitiously. Names, characters, and places are products of the author's imagination.

Front cover image by Suke Cerulo
Book design by Suke Cerulo
Cover Photo by Jessica Maceli
Inside/Back cover photo: Paul Citone
About Author Photo by Paul Citone
Student Reviewer Linda Ameroso

Printed by Lead Guitar Workshop, Inc., in the United States of America.

First edition 2021.

SCAN FOR MORE

for all backing tracks and videos

www.LeadGuitarWorkshop.com

PREFACE

I always enjoyed music as a kid but my immediate family was not musical. There wasn't a lot of music playing in the house and we were never the type of family to sing. But my Grandfather George Lane was a Big Band musician and bandleader in the 1950's in Boston and New York. I don't have any memories of him playing music but he would have hilarious stories "from the road" traveling with the band. Later in life I really learned to appreciate them as I toured extensively.

It was 1984 and I heard Van Halen for the first time. I knew right then and there that I wanted to play music. I got my first guitar for Christmas in that year and quickly took lessons because I had no idea what to do. At the time I was really into playing football and I was good at it. I realized I was never going to be in the NFL or make a career out of it. But I did realize there was no NFL of music, anybody could play! That was so exciting. I knew I was going to play music for my whole life. I just had to figure out how to make it a career.

I had weekly guitar lessons from the time I was twelve until I graduated High School. For most of this time my teacher was Sandy Prager. He played "third stream jazz" on a nylon string guitar. This was as far away from Van Halen as possible without being a classical guitarist. But I learned so much about music, how to think about it and improvise. He constantly had me creating. Once I finished High School I went to **Berklee College of Music**. It was the only school I wanted to go to. After four years I got my Bachelors Degree in Professional Music.

My one goal upon graduating was to join a band. Fortunately for me I met my future bandmates of 30 plus years. We formed the band "**Schleigho**" in 1993 and toured full time within a year or so. We toured 200 plus dates a year for almost five years straight and still play to this day. We recorded and released 5 albums. We signed a label with the **Allman Brothers Band**, toured with **Derek Trucks**, and played with so very many people all over the country. This was my "real world" music education.

But even though I had lessons in High School and a great experience at Berklee I still felt like I was slow learning and still really didn't get the true nature of music and guitar. I struggled to connect the musical dots.

I had to build confidence to make my own conclusions about music. I heard so many different ideas, terms, explanations and they were confusing. I was perplexed that music had been around for hundreds of years and there was still so much indecision about ideas and terminology.

I had to separate music from the instrument. This was one of my biggest realizations. It came into fruition when I started playing flute. I realized the music was its own language independent of the instrument that plays it. When I started really practicing flute my guitar playing got better! I was stunned, but I realized my musicianship was better and it was now translating to guitar.

Once my band started touring I had guitar players (and flute players) asking me for lessons. I think I gave my first lesson in 1995. It was very casual and it was new to me but I was just trying to help people out. I realized I had a good way of explaining things and I was able to connect with people. Over the years I kept teaching. It was rewarding and I was learning a lot by having to explain music to people in many different ways.

About six months after I moved to NYC in 2003 I got my first real teaching job at a guitar school in NYC. I was touring and teaching full time. I was engulfed in playing and teaching music and it was wonderful. As touring slowed down the teaching picked up. I was teaching ten classes and about thirty private students. Close to eighty folks a week were coming to see me to learn about guitar and music. After years of teaching groups and private students I was able to refine my approach to teaching and to understanding music and how it relates to the guitar. Years ago I estimated that I hit my 10,000 hours as a guitar player. Now I was hitting my 10,000 hours as a teacher.

In 2003 I wrote my first book "Lead Guitar Basics" for me to use at the guitar school. Over the years this grew into five complete books and a number of rewrites. I also became the Director of the Lead Guitar Department. I train other teachers to teach my material and musically evaluate all incoming teachers to the school.

I was amassing an unprecedented amount of teaching experience and gaining access to hundreds, if not thousands of guitar players struggling in the same way I had. Over years of refinement I was able to develop this entire pedagogy for learning lead guitar.

These books have three decades of experience behind them and seventeen years of in-classroom development. I believe in these books, and I think they will help you immensely as you become a better guitarist and musician. These are all the things I wish I had when I was starting my journey.

HOW TO USE BOOK

Each book is written as ten lessons continually building on each other. The books all work together and are meant to extend and expand your knowledge as you work and grow with them. Go through them in order and go back later to revisit topics.

These books were initially created as 10 week courses, one chapter per week. You can use it in the same way. Each Chapter is about an hour long. There are enough warm-ups, exercises, new skills and practice to last you for a week. There is overlap and repetition in the books to really help reinforce the core ideas.

Every lesson is structured the same way. It is meant to optimize your learning, efficiency, and time. The repetition creates good habits.

Tune in: First you have to get in the right head space. You must remind yourself that you are a musician and a guitar player. That music is Melody, Harmony, and Rhythm; and that rhythm is the number one factor to sounding good. It's like a mantra.

Warm-up: These are exercises to get your musical blood flowing and synchronize your internal clock. There are usually up to three warm-ups; *Muted String Ladders, Shells,* and *Changing Gears.* They are all music based and are like push-ups and jumping jacks to athletes.

Exercises: These are straight up music exercises like scales, arpeggios and more.

Review: This is part of the learning circle. You must review everything you learn. Eventually that will become part of your everyday language.

New Topic: Learn something new. It can be big or small, but it should expand your knowledge, even if it's learning something new about something you already know.

Practice: Play! Get better by playing music. Use your new idea/technique, concept in real time in the music you are playing, even if it is a one chord jam by yourself. Self Generating music and backing tracks are a focal point.

Summary: A reminder of what has been learned so far. Summaries compound with each chapter.

Going through each word and each note as written in these books is only part of the bigger picture. You have to imagine how music is working and how it relates to your instrument. You have to have a desire to grow and a never ending curiosity about music. If you keep questioning music you will find more answers and go deeper and deeper. You have to "drive" music, start a song yourself, jam on it and make it music all by yourself. When you're playing by yourself and someone walks in they should ask you "What song are you playing?" not "What are you practicing?" Learning music and playing is not about checking off a list of requirements. It's about sounding like a musician playing good music, and not someone noodling at the guitar store.

At a certain point in your musical life, you will learn all the information about music that you will ever use. Then your growth is about becoming closer to that information and growing deeper with it every time you revisit it. There isn't a learning path in music, it's a learning circle. An ever expanding circle is like rings in a tree. It's the growth in the rings, in the trunk of the tree that allows those branches to grow and extend.

Music is just a language and a guitar is just an instrument. Both are silent without you, you are music!

As guitarists Pat Martino and Mike Stern both told me, and I will tell you, "Just keep playing." Enjoy!

Suke Cerulo

Table of Contents

Lead Guitar-MODES

This book is for lead guitar players who feel comfortable with pentatonic scales and want to learn about the seven note scales. This book will build upon the knowledge of pentatonic scales so players can take full advantage of the modes. Learners will understand how keys are built and their subsequent chord progressions. As a guitar player you will discover all five patterns for your entire fretboard for any key and any mode. As a musician you will understand how every key is created and how to spell any mode. You will know when to use them and how they will sound as a result.

CHAPTER 1

TUNE IN

It is especially helpful to remind yourself that you will be learning on two different levels: as a musician and as a guitar player.

As a musician you will learn about keys and scales (specifically, the seven notes, seven chords, and seven modes in the Key of G). You will also learn how to relate that knowledge to the other eleven keys.

As a guitar player you will be learning the entire fretboard in the key of G including it's seven modes. Five patterns of seven notes and how to change keys and modes.

"I am a musician and a guitar player. Music is my language and my guitar is my voice. Music is Melody, Harmony and Rhythm. I develop my language skills and my instrument skills. They are two separate worlds working together to complete the circle of music."

Rhythm is the number one factor to sounding great as a musician.

MUSICAL TRUTHS

Think like a musician first. Here are a few MUSICAL TRUTHS.

- There are 12 notes in all of music. Seven of them are A B C D E F G known as the "natural" notes.

- Sharp (#) raises a note/chord/scale by a half-step.

- Flat (b) lowers a note/chord/scale by half-step.

- Sharped and flattened notes are know as "accidentals" and they have two names. For example F# is also Gb.

- There are 7 Natural notes and 5 Accidentals to make 12 total notes.

- A half-step (H) in music is the smallest distance between notes. (1 fret)

- A whole-step (W) is two half-steps. (2 frets)

- All notes are a whole-step (2 frets) apart except BC and EF which are half-steps. (1 fret) (true with open strings too)

- The 12 notes are always in the same order going up and down. (especially true on any/all guitar strings)

- There are 12 keys in music, one based on each note.

- Each key is a Major scale based on the formula **W W H W W W H.**

- Each Key has 7 chords, one for each note.
  Uppercase = Major, *lower case* = minor, the last chord is *diminished*.
  The formula for the chords in ALL keys is:

WHAT IS A MODE?

Modes are functions of a scale and Modes are chord progressions

MODES AS SCALES

Modes are the seven note Major scale (WWHWWWH) established as seven different scales, one starting on each one of its own seven tones.

What we know as the "Major scale" is the first mode known as IONIAN. What we call the "minor scale" is the sixth mode known as AEOLIAN. These are the Relative Major and minors of the key. There are five more modes based on the other five notes.

When the Major scale starts with (and resolves to) another note in that scale it creates a variation of a major or minor scale. Each has a different sound because of the locations of the two half-steps in the scale. This creates three Major modes, three minor modes and a diminished mode.

Here is the first mode IONIAN starting from G using the formula WWHWWWH

W		W		H	W		W		W		H	
G	G#	A	A#	B	C	C#	D	D#	E	F	F#	G

Listen to the G Ionian scale, starting with G. When you play this scale starting from the A or B instead, the formula shifts and the scale sounds radically different. This happens for each of the notes creating seven modes, giving them each a unique sound even though they are the same notes. This will be discussed further in later chapters.

G		A		B	C		D		E		F#	G
A		B	C		D		E		F#	G		A
B	C		D		E		F#	G		A		B

MODES AS CHORD PROGRESSIONS

Modes as chord progressions was such a huge revelation to me. For years they were only taught to me as scales, musically and as a guitar player. But after playing 1000's of songs and teaching even more, I realized that the modes were happening because of the chords and specifically which chord was resolved to. In the last 100 years there has been a ton of music that started with someone playing chords first and singing second in response to the chord progression.

There are seven chords in a key, one for each note. Based on the "Rule of Thirds" (stacking every other note) you create a TRIAD (three note chord) from each of the notes in the scale to create these seven chords. This results in three Major chords, three minor chords and one diminished chord.

In music we use upper-case Roman numerals for Major chords and lower-case for minor chords. The small circle is used for diminished. Here is the master formula, the DIATONIC HARMONY formula for all 12 keys:

$$\text{I} \quad \text{ii} \quad \text{iii} \quad \text{IV} \quad \text{V} \quad \text{vi} \quad \text{vii}^{\circ}$$

This formula is one of the most important things to know as a musician. Along with the names of the 12 notes and WWHWWWH this can get you through most of your music life. We will dig deeper into this in later chapters. But for now you need to know the formula. Here are some observations.

1. The I, IV, V are Major chords.
2. The ii, iii, vi are minor chords.
3. The vii is diminished.
4. The relative Major is I.
5. The relative minor is vi.
6. There are ONLY THREE Major chords per key.
7. There are ONLY THREE minor chords per key.

Each chord has a mode associated with it and it shares its quality too (Major or minor or diminished). The modes are always in the same order in a key, just as the notes and the chords. The only difference is which note/chord is the "MAIN" note, the TONIC.

NAME	DEGREE		TYPE/CHORD	
Ionian	1	I	MAJOR	Relative MAJOR
Dorian	2	ii	minor	
Phrygian	3	iii	minor	
Lydian	4	IV	MAJOR	
Mixolydian	5	V	MAJOR	
Aeolian	6	vi	minor	Relative minor
Locrian	7	vii°	*diminished	not common

CHORDS IN CONTEXT

When deciding which key you are in and what the main chord is -It's all about context, . Once you know the Diatonic Harmony formula, you know to look for certain things, like three major chords, and two of them are alphabetically next to each other. Below is a typical G Major chord progression using the I, IV and V chords (G, C, D). If you strum it a few times you would definitely want to end on the G chord.

But what if the order of the chords were changed? Now the D chord is the main chord. Same three chords, and they can only come from the key of G. This is not the key of D. (Key of D has C# note and C# is a diminished chord.) This is a MODE from the fifth chord in the key of G, called D MIXOLYDIAN. It uses the chords in the key but the fifth chord is the "main" chord. In this case the D chord acts as the tonic.

$$\frac{4}{4}|D \qquad |C \quad G \quad \|$$

ANY CHORD IN A KEY CAN BE THE "MAIN" CHORD OF A PROGRESSION.
THESE ARE THE MODES.

OCTAVES

A a guitar player it is essential to see how octaves live on the fretboard.

On the left are the Neck Anatomy octaves, both SHORT and LONG. These are the keystone to unlocking your fretboard as a three octave instrument.

On the right are the "Behind" octaves. They skip two strings and go backwards (musically up but the hand goes down the neck). These shapes are most helpful when in a pattern.

The Behind Octaves happen in your old school C chord and small bar F chord, and even the open G chord.

These are all the same on any fret and especially true regarding the open strings.

Octaves are the pathway to seeing all of the notes on your fretboard.

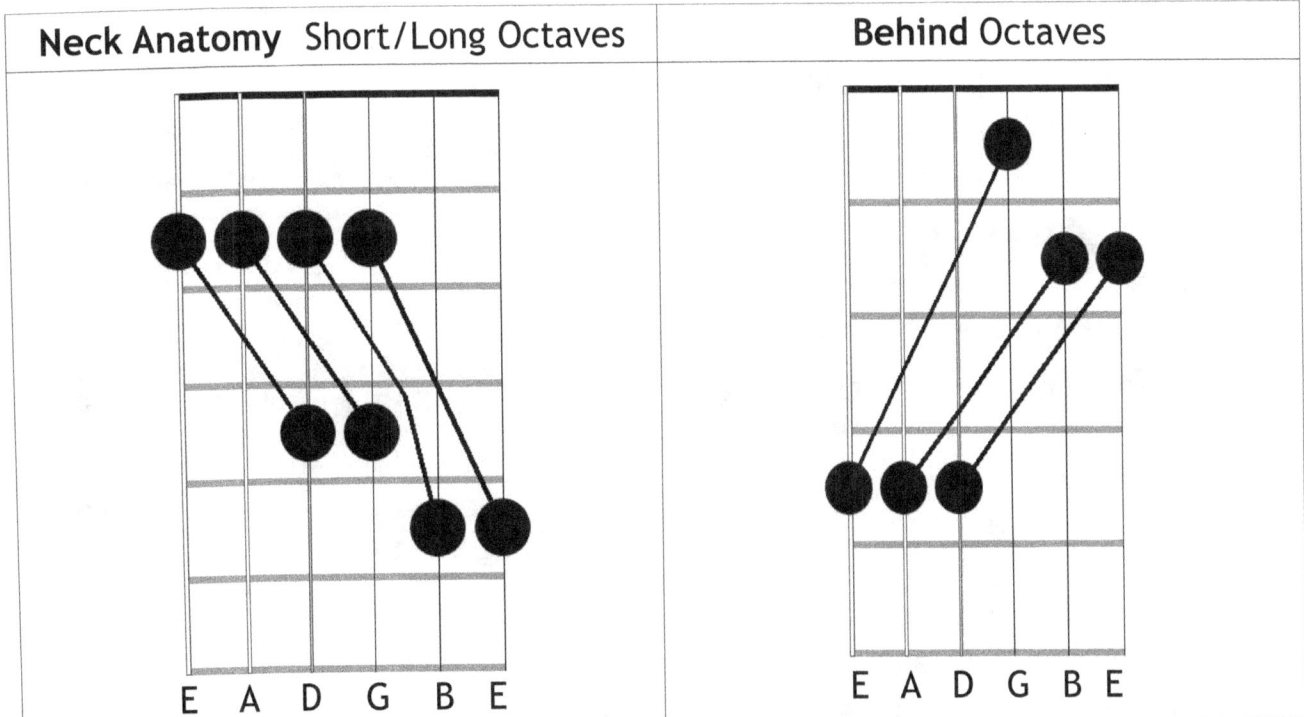

| Neck Anatomy Short/Long Octaves | Behind Octaves |

E A D G B E   E A D G B E

PATTERN #1 - Key of G

Pattern #1 is the same as the pentatonic. The pentatonic has 5 notes and the Key of G has seven notes. Musically we are adding a C and F# note. If counting from G these would add the 4th and 7th degrees to the scale. In the key of G, pattern #1 is in the OPEN position and starts again, an octave higher on the 12th fret.

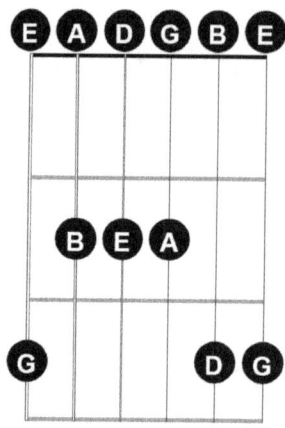

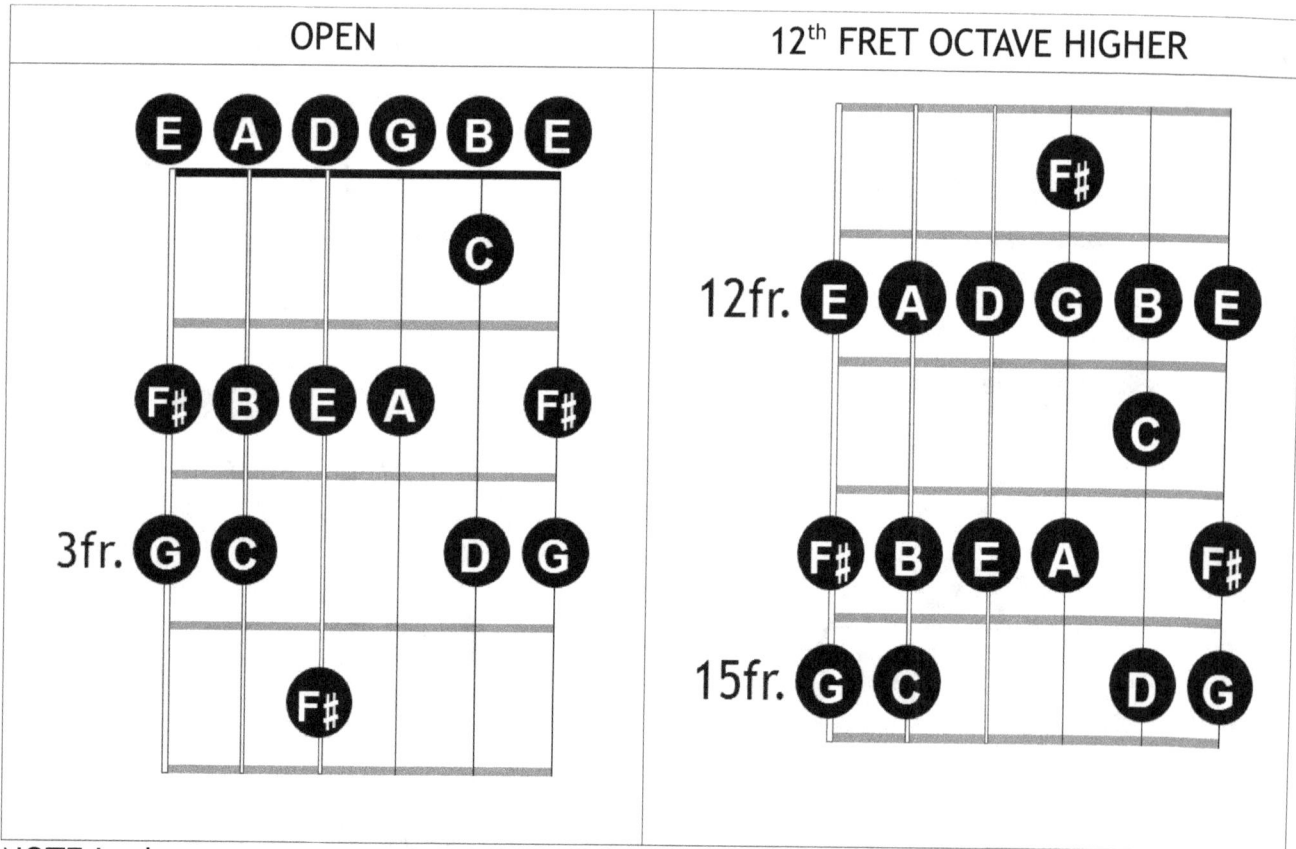

NOTE In the open pattern the F# on the G string has to be relocated to the D string.

PRACTICE

SELF-GENERATING (SELF-GEN) with one bar G Chord then one bar 8th notes G Ionian scale in pattern #1. One octave at a time ascending and descending.

IONIAN

Ionian is an extremely common sound. It's Major! It is the first MODE in a key. It's the foundation of our music. Ionian is the same as the "The Key of X Major."

In the key of G Major: **G A B C D E F# G**

Here are some common chord progressions. On the left are the names of the chords in the Key of G. On the right is the relationship in terms of degree. As long as the song *resolves* to the G chord and only uses chords in the key it will be G Ionian.

CHORD PROGRESSION	CHORD RELATIONSHIP
|G |C |	I IV
|G |D |	I V
|G |C D |	I IV V
|G C |D G |	I IV V I
|G C |G D |	I IV I V
|G Em |C D |	I vi IV V
|G D |Em C |	I V vi IV

BACKING TRACK

G Ionian Backing track.

| G | D | Em | C | |

PLAY ALONG BACKING TRACK
www.LeadGuitarWorkshop.com

LICKS

Here are eight licks in G Ionian in Pattern #1 in the open position. These are flexible and malleable. Most of them can be divided in half, allowing you to start them on beat three of a bar instead of beat one.

Licks are little bits of conversation. You can manipulate them in any way you want and of course you can make up and find your own. The better you get at improvising the less you will think about them and just let them flow.

Play them over the BACKING TRACK or by SELF GENERATING. They are not meant to be played straight through (although that works). Each one is a seed for similar ideas that expand from the first. Change a note, change the rhythm, add hammer-ons and pull-offs, anything that sounds cool.

SUMMARY

We are musicians. We are guitar players.
We learn the language of music. Melody, Harmony, and Rhythm
We learn the craft of playing the guitar as an instrument.

We warm up with Muted String Ladders (MSL) and SHELLS.

RHYTHM is most important.

MODES are a function of a scale. You can start any scale on any one of its own notes.

The names of the MODES: **Ionian, Dorian, Phrygian, Lydian, Mixolydian, Aeolian, Locrian.**

MODES are CHORD PROGRESSIONS. You can use any of the chords in a key to be the "main" chord, the TONIC.

Diatonic Harmony = $\text{I} \quad \text{ii} \quad \text{iii} \quad \text{IV} \quad \text{V} \quad \text{vi} \quad \text{vii}^{\circ}$

In the Key of G, G is Ionian and is spelled **G A B C D E F# G** based on WWHWWWH from the G note. It also has a G Major chord.

As guitar players it is extremely helpful to see your octaves.

For the key of G Major, we learned how to add two notes (C and F#) to our scale pattern by filling in the pentatonic pattern #1.

Don't forget that at the 12th fret the guitar (an music world) starts over again an octave higher. That means for the Keys of G (12th-15th fret) up to D (19th-22nd fret) you get Pattern #1 an octave higher.

We use BACKING TRACKS and SELF GENERATE to give a real time context to our playing.

We still use PATTERN #1 Rock and Roll Rule to navigate our scales and to easily see the relationship between the Relative Major and Relative minor.

CHAPTER 2

TUNE IN

"I am a musician and a guitar player. Music is my language and my guitar is my voice. Music is Melody, Harmony and Rhythm. I develop my language skills and my instrument skills. They are two separate worlds working together to complete the circle of music."

Rhythm is the number one factor to sounding great as a musician.

WARM UP

Muted String Ladder   ALL DOWNS   ALL UPS   ALL ALTERNATE in EACH GEAR

SHELLS

Dexterity exercises to help practice common groups of notes as well as overcome any fingering problems.

- **FINGERING** - For example, 1 2 4 ascend and descend, then reverse 4 2 1 ascend and descend
- **PERFORMANCE** - Play in position (same fret)
- **RHYTHM** - eighth-notes (ultimately play all gears, quarter-notes, eighth-notes, triplets and sixteenths)

SHELL 2 4

SHELL 1 2 4

EXERCISE

Descending and Ascending Pattern #1

Highest note to lowest note in pattern and back. No musical considerations, just full pattern practice. Ultimately do in all gears.

Self-Gen G Ionian   Eighth-notes descending and ascending

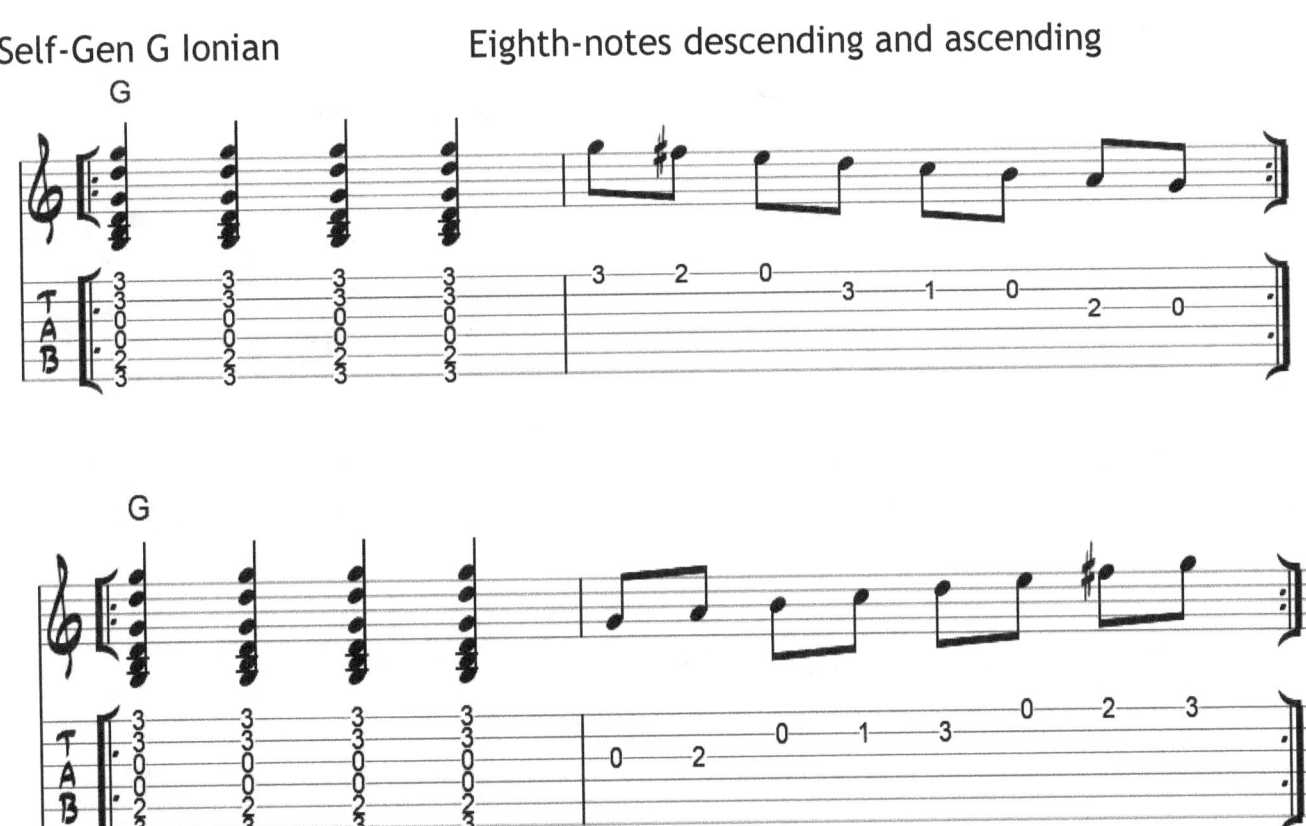

Self-Gen licks in G Ionian
Each lick is its own. Repeat any one or play them in any order.
Create your own.

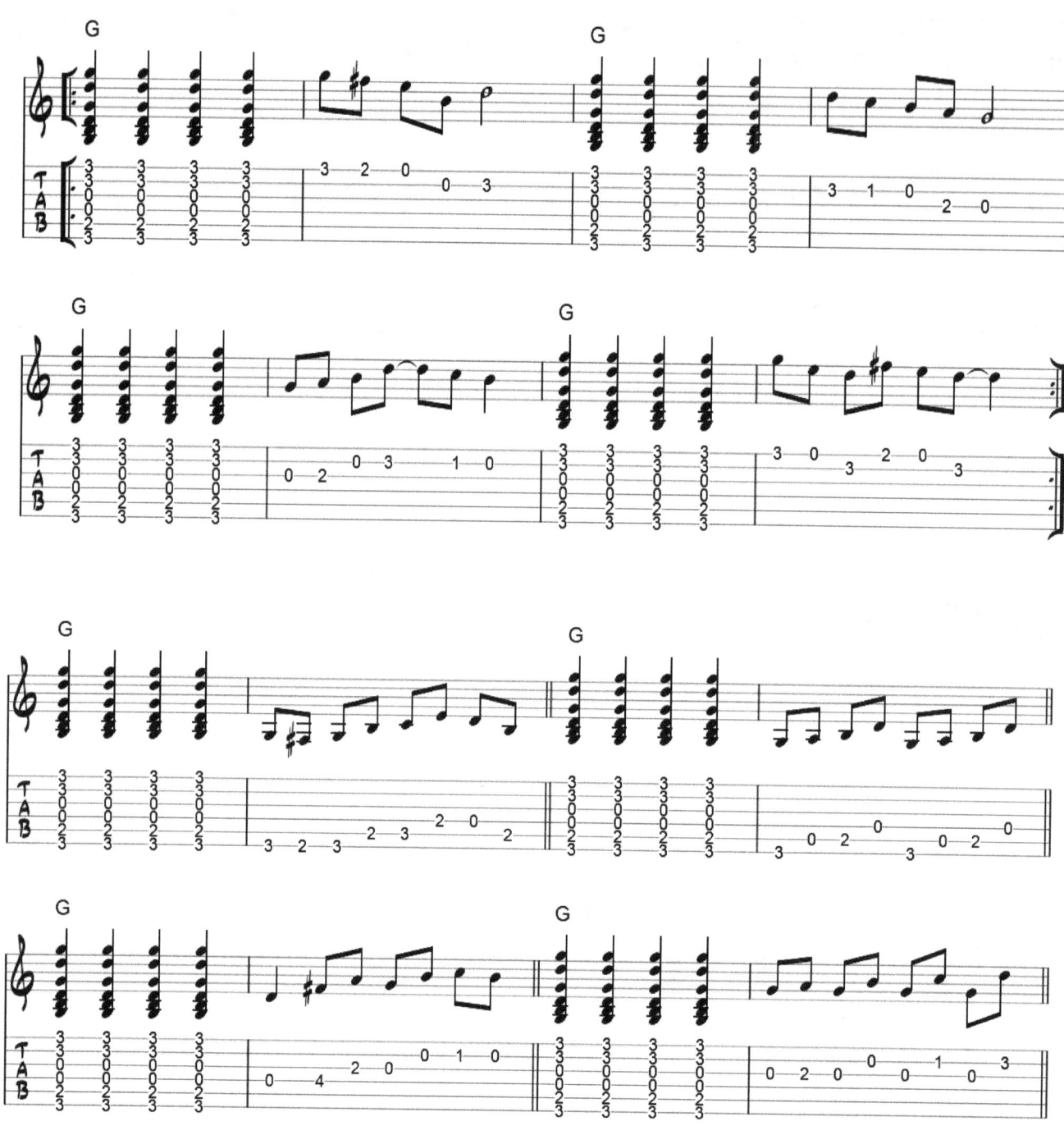

REVIEW

Modes happen in our world in two ways. We hear them as scales, melodic sounds starting and resolving to any note in the scale. We also hear them as the resulting chord progression. Chords! Starting and resolving on any chord in the key, not just the relative Major and minor.

We are dealing with these two ways, as a musician and a guitar player. As a musician we learn about the Diatonic Harmony formula to know the quality of the chords in any of our 12 keys. We learn how to recognize a mode by its chord progression. We also learn them as scales, to solo with and make melodies.

As a guitar player we have to learn how to map out the seven notes of a key on our guitar. We learn the 5 patterns based on our pentatonics and add two notes to each pattern. We learn to see the octaves on our fretboard to find the root of any mode in any pattern.

There are also different ways modes happen in music. One is just by virtue of a song being in a key with a scale and chords that go with it. Almost every song is in a mode in some way. Simple G to C songs with a melody are probably in G Ionian, even if the artist wasn't thinking anything at all about theory. For example the verse to "Last Dance with Mary Jane" by Tom Petty is A Dorian (Am G D Am). I don't think Tom Petty was thinking of anything but the story and mood when he wrote that song.

The other way modes happen in music is when musicians take advantage of the sound of a mode and usually play a few chords repeatedly and solo for longer lengths of time. Jazz is very much at home in this. Miles Davis started doing this in the 50's to break free from the traditional format of the old jazz tunes. This led to a complete change in the jazz world that then started overflowing into the rock world with bands like the Grateful Dead, Jimi Hendrix and the Allman Brothers. Guitar players started taking longer and deeper solos, again exploiting the sounds that modes offer.

DORIAN

Dorian is the second mode in a key and is based on the second chord. Both are minor. Dorian is an extremely common mode that I call the "Happy minor". Dorian is the first of the three minor modes (ii, iii, vi). Remember the modes match the chords in the key. There are also three Major modes (Ionian was one) and a half-diminished mode (the last).

The scale is: A B C D E F# G

People love Dorian, although it is a minor scale based on the **ii** minor chord (Am in our key). Dorian has an upbeat, groovy and happy sound to it. I would say it is as equally popular as "the minor" Aeolian. It's a great combination of getting the endearing sound of minor but with the sound of hope.

CHORD PROGRESSION	CHORD RELATIONSHIP - *AS IS* CHORD RELATIONSHIP - *TRADITIONAL**
|Am |D |	ii V i IV*
|Am |Bm |	ii iii i ii*
|Am |C D |	ii IV V i bIII IV*
|Am |G D |	ii I V i bVII IV*
|Am D |Em |	ii V vi i IV v*
|Am Bm |C Bm |	ii iii IV iii i ii bIII ii*

Traditional notation requires you start the numbering on the "main" chord and then adjust the intervals accordingly. **Am** becomes the "one" chord and the G is a W step below, so it's considered a flat seven away. It's complicated.

PRACTICE

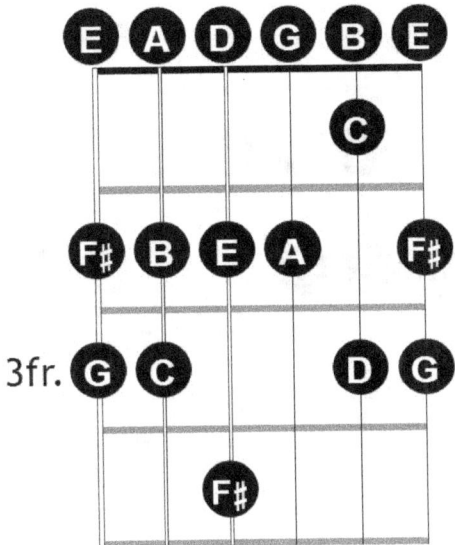

A Dorian scale in Pattern #1

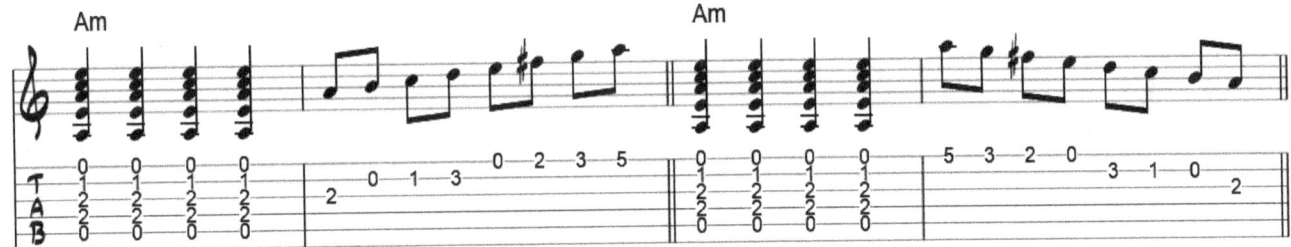

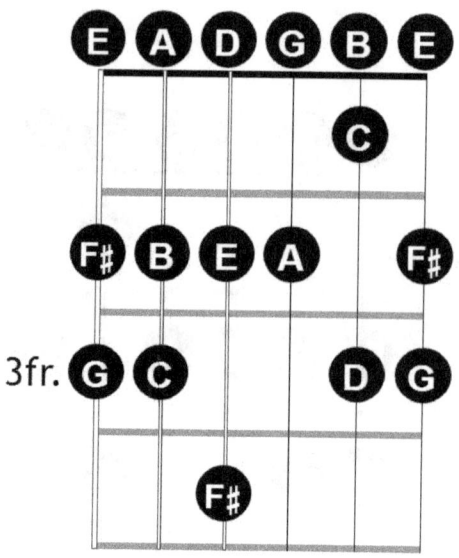

A Dorian Licks in Pattern #1

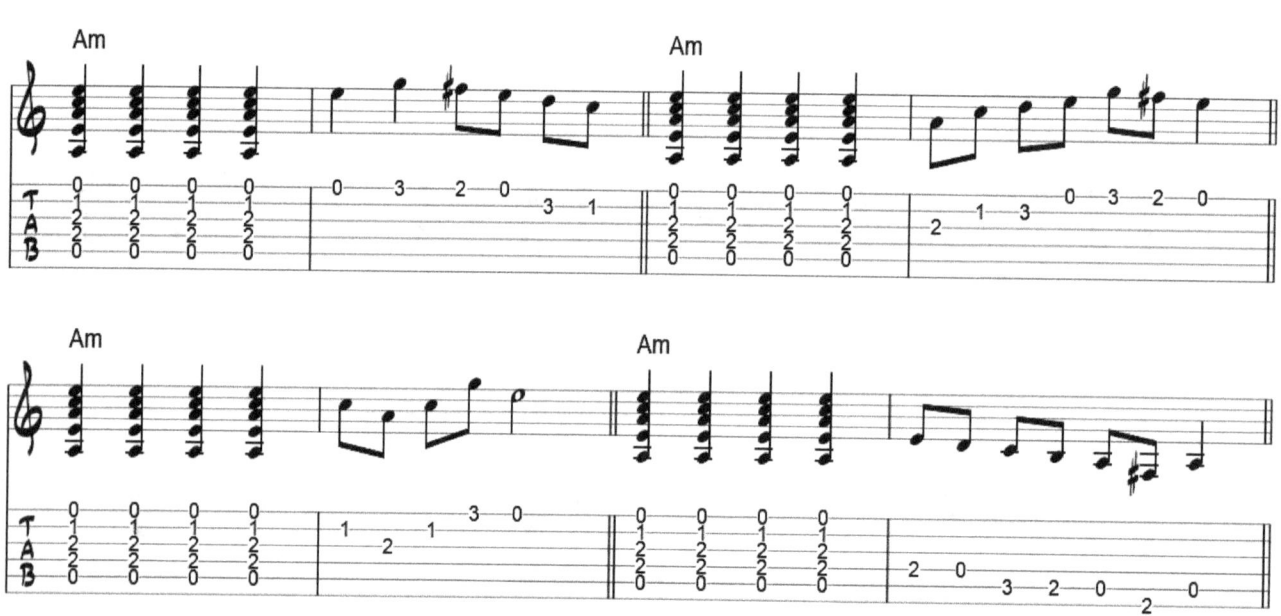

PATTERN #2

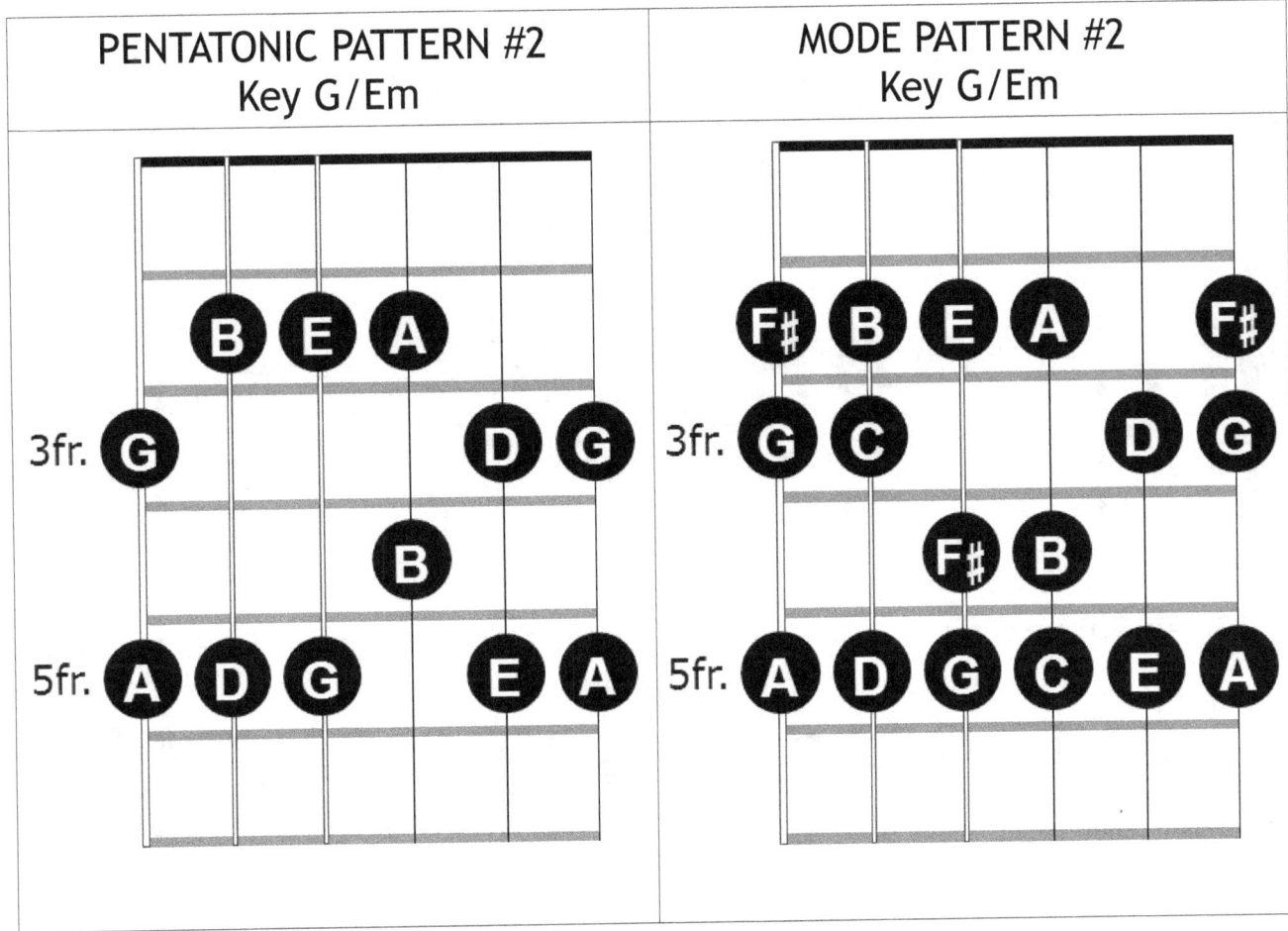

| PENTATONIC PATTERN #2
Key G/Em | MODE PATTERN #2
Key G/Em |

Pentatonic scales can be thought of as relating to the chord and to the key. When thinking the mode pattern you would think of the "parental" key to access all the modes properly. Map out the 5 patterns of the pentatonic scale for the key (G/Em) and then add the 2 notes into the scale.

Then, as a musician, you use all 5 patterns to play the 7 modes in the key of G: G Ionian, A Dorian, B Phrygian, C Lydian, D Mixolydian, E Aeolian and F# Locrian.

It's important to note that you can apply any chords pentatonic directly. Meaning, in A Dorian you can revert back to A minor pentatonic. Similarly, in D Mixolydian you can use D Major pentatonic. This always works when you match the pentatonic to the chord directly.

PATTERN #2 PRACTICE

G Ionian Pattern #2   Two Octaves ascending and descending

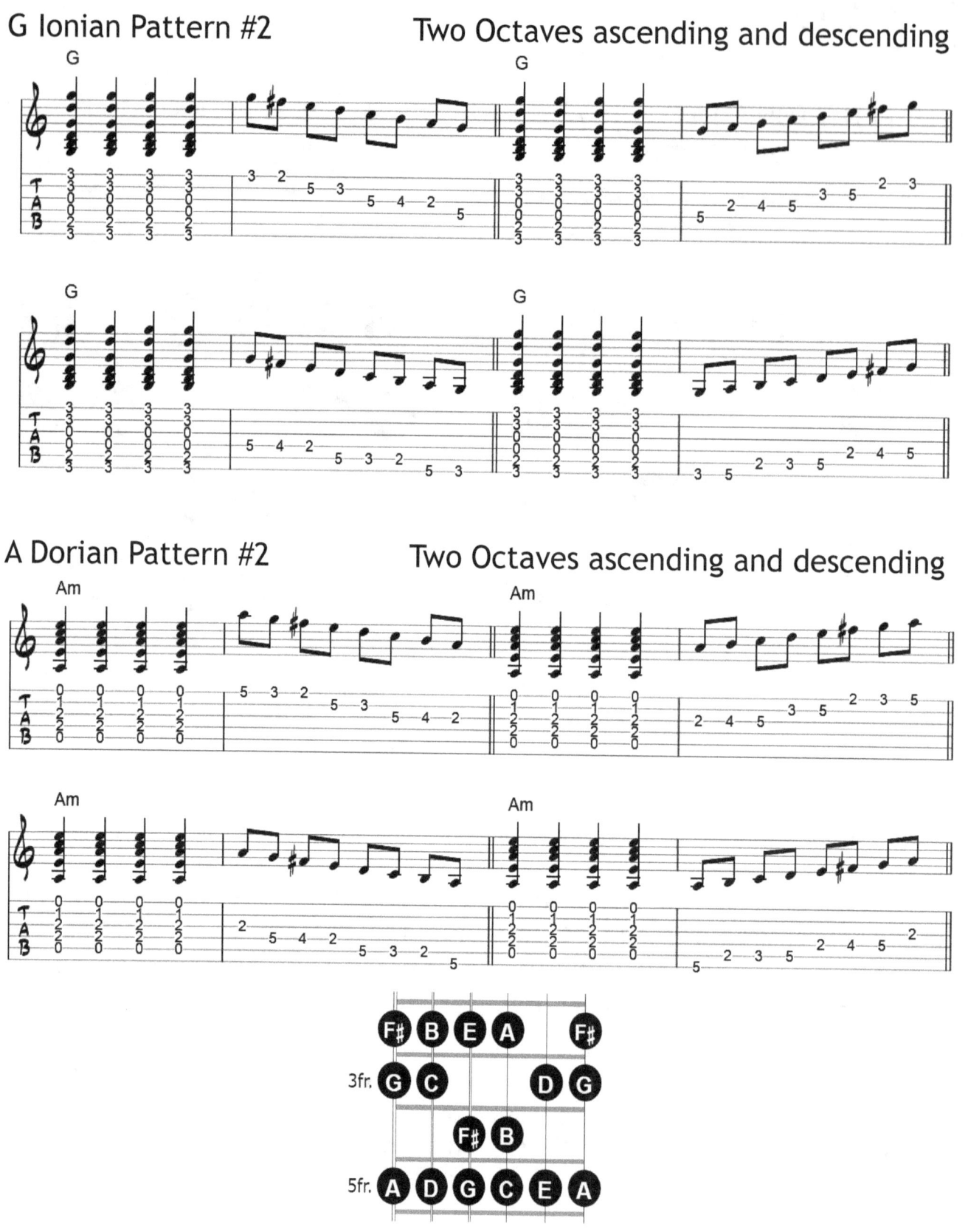

A Dorian Pattern #2   Two Octaves ascending and descending

| Am |D |

PLAY ALONG BACKING TRACK
www.LeadGuitarWorkshop.com

LICKS

A Dorian-Pattern #1 licks

SAME LICKS IN PATTERN #2 (A Dorian)

A Dorian Pattern #2 extra licks

SUMMARY

We are musicians. We are guitar players.
We learn the language of music. Melody, Harmony, and Rhythm
We learn the craft of playing the guitar as an instrument.

We warm up with Muted String Ladders (MSL) and SHELLS.

RHYTHM is most important.

MODES are a function of a scale. You can start any scale on any one of its own notes.

The names of the MODES: **Ionian, Dorian, Phrygian, Lydian, Mixolydian, Aeolian, Locrian.**

MODES are CHORD PROGRESSIONS. You can use any of the chords in a key to be the "main" chord, the TONIC.

We learn to see common modal chord progressions.

Diatonic Harmony = **I ii iii IV V vi vii°**

As guitar players it is extremely helpful to see your octaves.

We learned how to add two notes (C and F#) to our scale pattern by filling in the pentatonic pattern #1 and pattern #2.

You will use Pattern #1 and #2 for ALL 12 Keys, one for each fret.

Don't forget that at the 12th fret the guitar (an music world) starts over again an octave higher.

We use BACKING TRACKS and SELF GENERATE to give a real time context to our playing.

ALL 5 PATTERNS SOUND THE SAME (depending on the mode you are in).
THEY ARE THE SAME SEVEN NOTES. They help you use your whole fretboard.

CHAPTER 3

TUNE IN

"I am a musician and a guitar player. Music is my language and my guitar is my voice. Music is Melody, Harmony and Rhythm. I develop my language skills and my instrument skills. They are two separate worlds working together to complete the circle of music."

Rhythm is the number one factor to sounding great as a musician.

WARM UP

Muted String Ladders   6 strings all alternate pick

EXERCISE

<u>Patterns #1 and 2</u>   descending and ascending   Eighth-notes

This is just pattern exercise, not thinking music responsibilities.

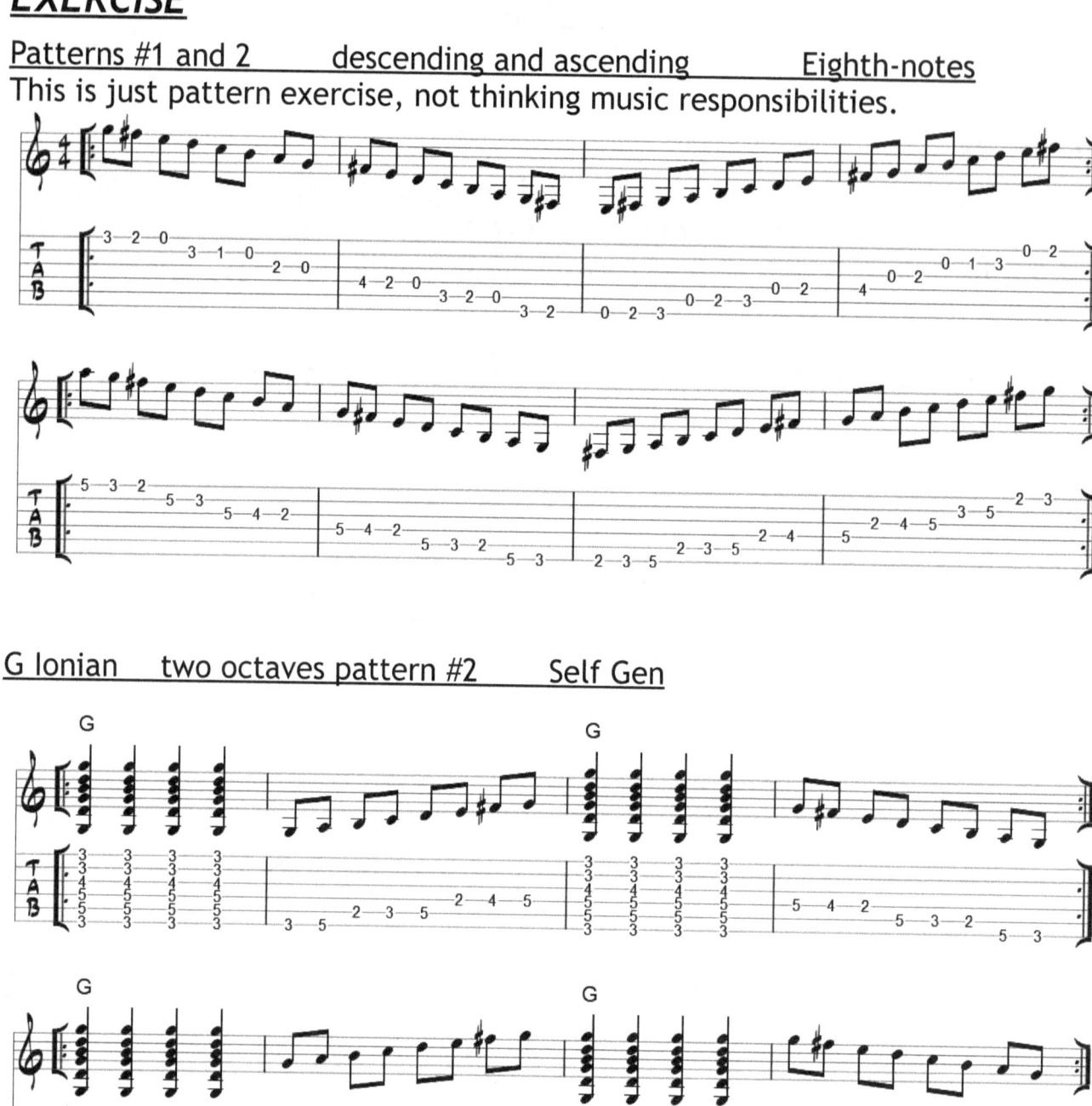

<u>G Ionian</u>   two octaves pattern #2   Self Gen

A Dorian   two octaves pattern #1   Self Gen

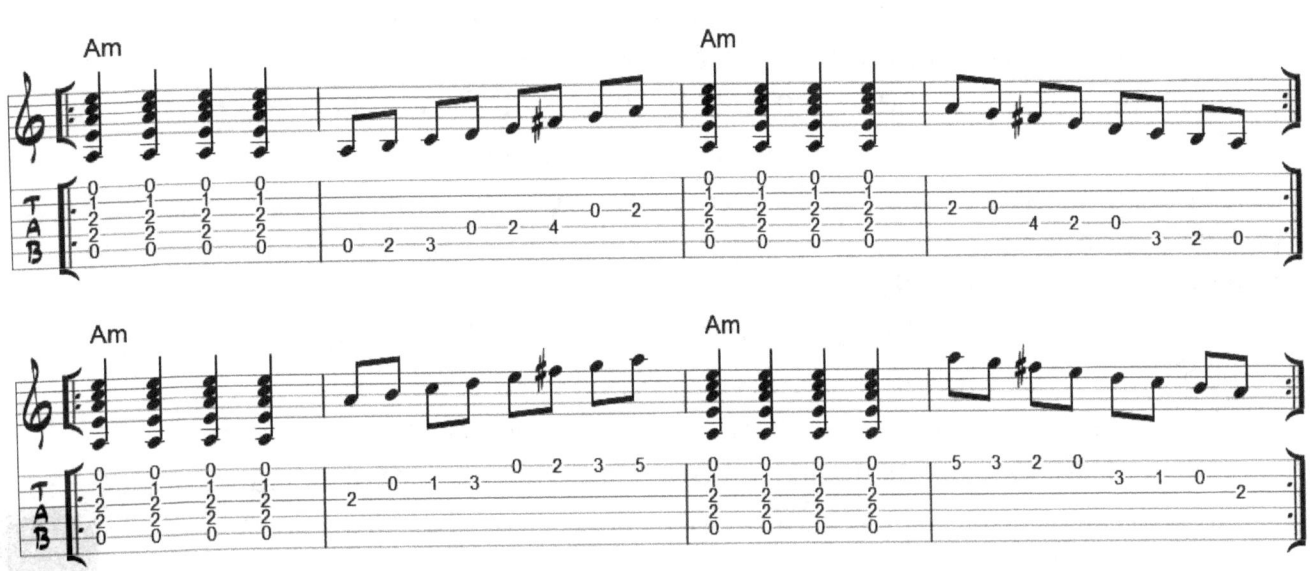

A Dorian   two octaves pattern #2   Self Gen

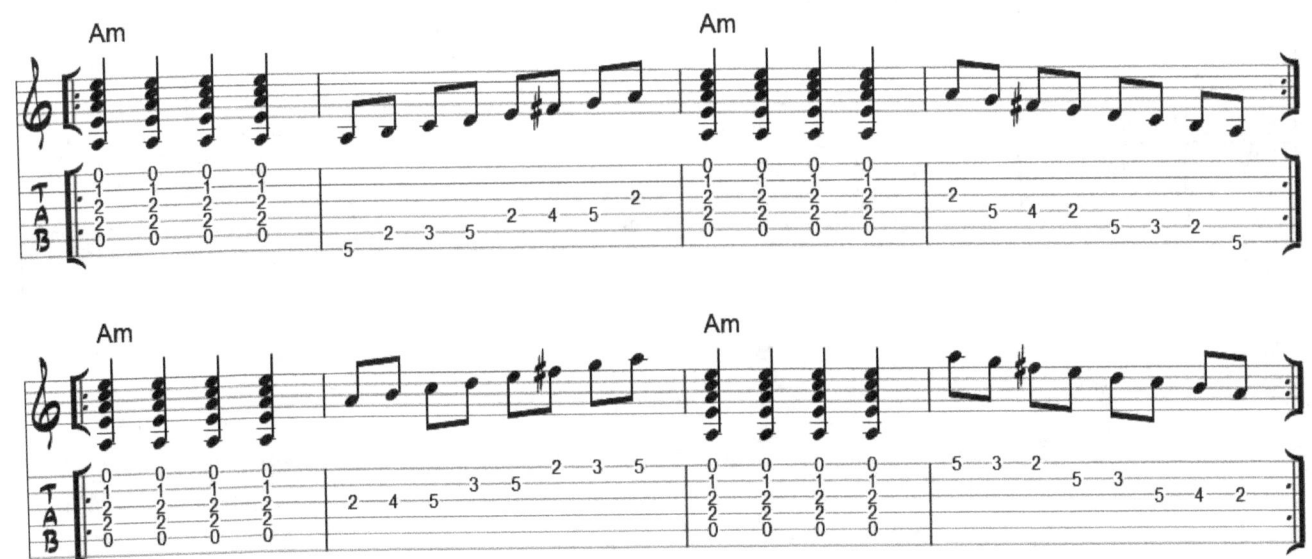

DIATONIC HARMONY

When you take a note and apply WWHWWWH to it you create the Major scale (Ionian). You then stack every other note for a total of three notes to create a triad. You do this for each note and you get the seven chords for the key that are the same names as the seven notes. The result is our Diatonic Formula:

I ii iii IV V vi vii*dim*

When you apply this to every key you get every note of every key, every chord and every mode. **You get all the keys, scales and notes in all of our traditional musical world.**

- The top row is our Diatonic Harmony formula for TRIADS.
- Below that is the same but for SEVENTH CHORDS.
- Below that are the names of the MODES, always in the same order.
- Below that are the traditional name and function of the scale by DEGREE
- SOUNDS lists my terms or descriptions on how the key sounds.
- ALL 12 KEYS reading down is circle of 5ths, up is the circle of 4ths.
- There are THREE MAJOR and THREE MINOR CHORDS per key.
- There are SIX very usable MODES in any key.

Triads	I	ii	iii	IV	V	vi	vii dim
	I Major	ii minor	iii minor	IV Major	V Major	vi minor	vii dim
7th Chords	I Maj7	iim7	iiim7	IV Maj7	V7	vim7	vii-7b5
Modes	Ionian	Dorian	Phrygian	Lydian	Mixolydian	Aeolian	Locrian
DEGREE	TONIC	SUPER TONIC	MEDIANT	SUB DOMINANT	DOMINANT	SUB MEDIANT	LEADING TONE
SOUND	Relative MAJOR*	Happy minor	Dark+Heavy minor	Exotic Major	Funky Major	Relative MINOR*	dark and dim
KEYS	C	D	E	F	G	A	B
5ths	G	A	B	C	D	E	F#
↓	D	E	F#	G	A	B	C#
	A	B	C#	D	E	F#	G#
	E	F#	G#	A	B	C#	D#
	B	C#	D#	E	F#	G#	A#
	Gb/F#	Ab/G#	Bb/A#	Cb/B	Db/C#	Eb/D#	F/E#
	Db	Eb	F	Gb	Ab	Bb	C
	Ab	Bb	C	Db	Eb	F	G
	Eb	F	G	Ab	Bb	C	D
↑	Bb	C	D	Eb	F	G	A
4ths	F	G	A	Bb	C	D	E

PHRYGIAN

Phrygian is the third mode and is a minor mode that goes with the iii minor chord in the key. For the Key of G that is a B minor chord, resulting in B Phrygian (**B C D E F# G A B**)

As a sound, Phrygian is the darkest of the three minor modes. Much of this has to do with the scale starting with a half-step (B to C). This adds a tremendous amount of tension and further darkens this minor scale. The mood of the scale falls between flamenco and metal.

As a mode Phrygian is definitely the least used of the three minor modes. (Dorian and Aeolian are the two other minor modes.). The unique fact that this mode starts with a half-step makes it very tricky to write melodies. Also, in a traditional sense, the Phrygian mode doesn't have a proper "V" chord. Traditionally in any mode the main chord is the "I" chord. For it to resolve properly it needs a "V" chord. The V to I is the strongest resolution is music. In Phrygian the "V" chord is the F# diminished chord. Therefore it's even more difficult to write a chord progression in Phrygian.

CHORD PROGRESSION	CHORD RELATIONSHIP - *AS IS* CHORD RELATIONSHIP - *TRADITIONAL**
|Bm |C |	iii IV i *b*II*
|Bm |C D |	iii IV V i *b*II *b*III*
|Bm C |Bm D |	iii IV iii V i *b*II I *b*III*
|Bm C |Em D |	iii IV vi V i *b*II iv *b*III*
|Bm Em |Am Bm |	iii vi ii iii i iv *b*vii i*
|Bm G |D Am |	iii I V ii i *b*VI *b*III *b*vi*

PATTERN #3

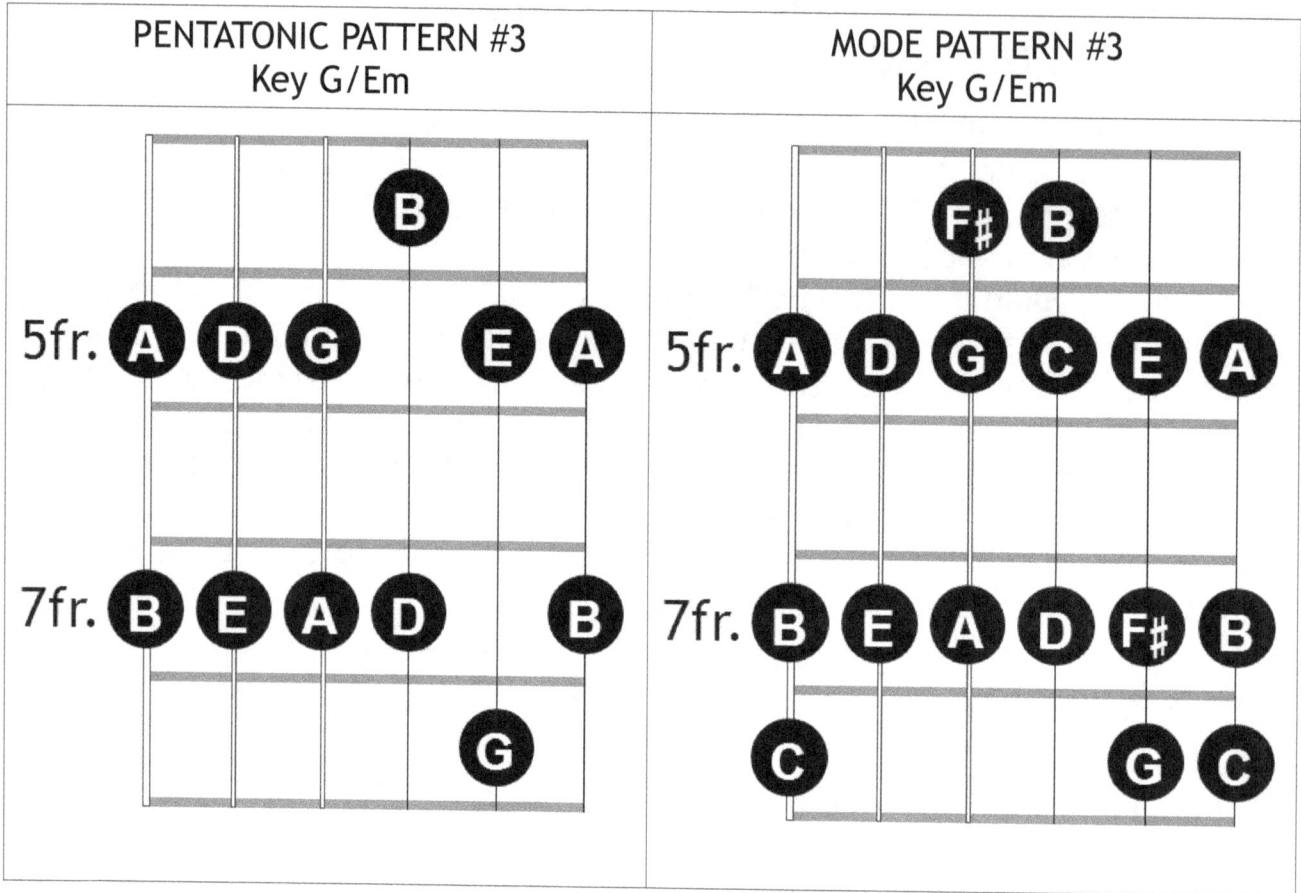

| PENTATONIC PATTERN #3 Key G/Em | MODE PATTERN #3 Key G/Em |

Remember that we are filling in the pentatonics of the KEY of G to access all seven notes of that key by adding the half-steps C and F#.

All seven notes are the modes: G Ionian, A Dorian, B Phrygian, C Lydian, D Mixolydian, E Aeolian, and F# Locrian.

Each pattern is two octaves of the same seven notes. As a guitar player the five patterns will allow us to use our entire fretboard for any key and any mode, allowing us the full range of our instrument (about 3 octaves).

As a musician, it is our responsibility to musically take full advantage of those seven notes, and to recognize chord progressions in a mode and use its matching scale to create different sounding melodies.

PRACTICE

Pattern #3 Ascending and Descending   Full range pattern only

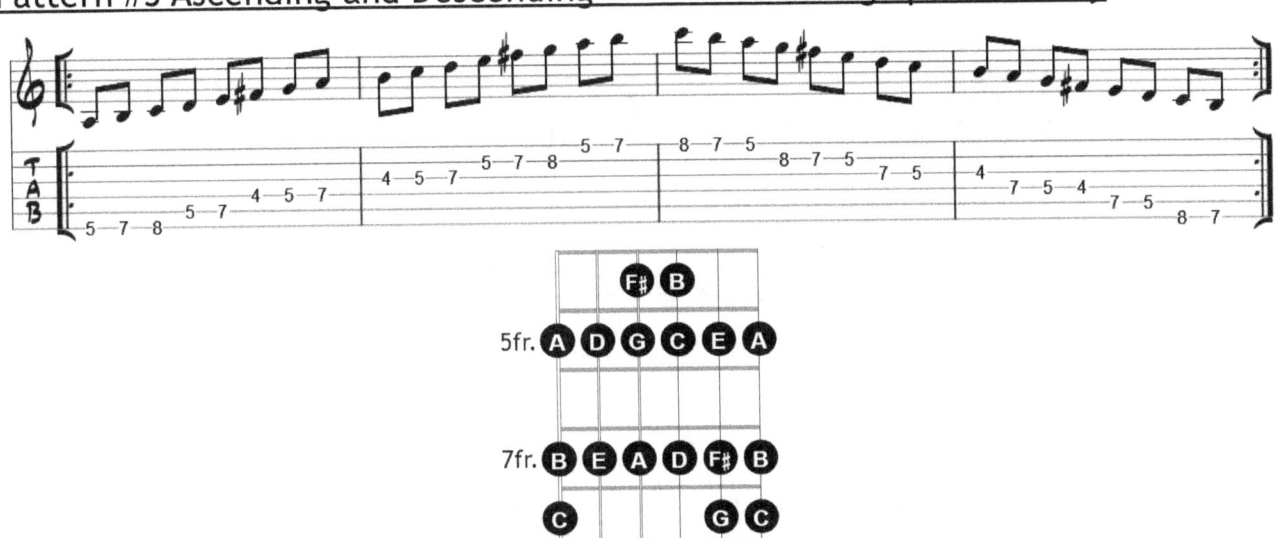

Self-Gen Pattern #3 G Ionian A Dorian B Phrygian 1 Octave ascend + descend

BACKING TRACK

| Bm | C | |

PLAY ALONG BACKING TRACK
www.LeadGuitarWorkshop.com

LICKS

Here are 4 licks in pattern #1 for B Phrygian. Followed by the same exact licks in Pattern #2 and Pattern #3. This helps with your ear matching your fingers and not getting hung up because of a given pattern. This also further illustrates how any one scale pattern is the same as the others. They all have the same seven notes, and any mode scale is in any pattern.

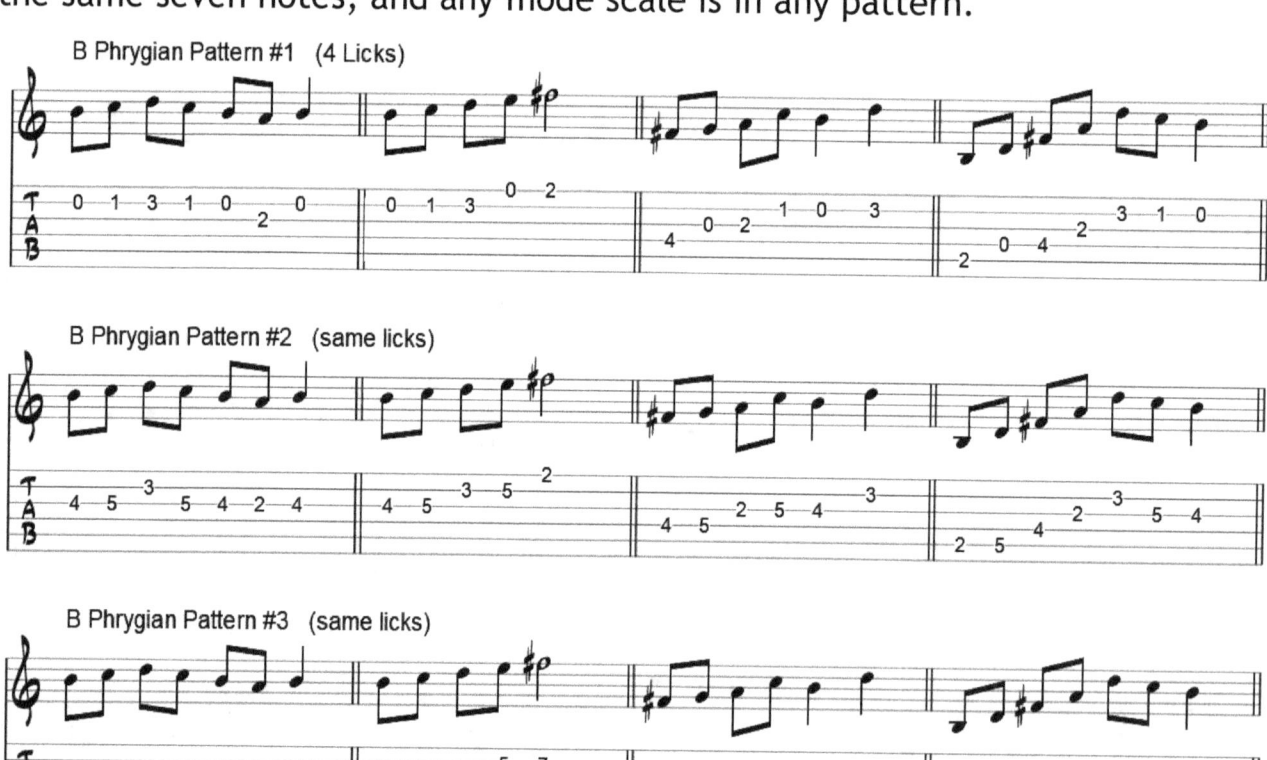

SUMMARY

We are musicians. We are guitar players.
We learn the language of music. Melody, Harmony, and Rhythm.
We learn the craft of playing the guitar as an instrument.

MODES are a function of a scale. You can start any scale on any one of its own notes.

The MODES are: **Ionian, Dorian, Phrygian, Lydian, Mixolydian, Aeolian, Locrian.**

MODES are CHORD PROGRESSIONS. You can use any of the chords in a key to be the "main" chord, the TONIC.

We learn to see common modal chord progressions.

Diatonic Harmony = **I ii iii IV V vi vii°**

As guitar players it is extremely helpful to see your octaves.

We learned how to add two notes (C and F#) to our scale pattern by filling in the pentatonic pattern #1 and pattern #2.

You will use Pattern #1, #2 and #3 for ALL 12 Keys, one for each fret. The three patterns are always connected and in the same order, always.

Don't forget that at the 12th fret the guitar (an music world) starts over again an octave higher.

We use BACKING TRACKS and SELF GENERATE to give a real time context to our playing.

ALL 5 PATTERNS SOUND THE SAME (depending on the mode). THEY ARE THE SAME SEVEN NOTES IN ANY GIVEN KEY.

CHAPTER 4

TUNE IN

"I am a musician and a guitar player. Music is my language and my guitar is my voice. Music is Melody, Harmony and Rhythm. I develop my language skills and my instrument skills. They are two separate worlds working together to complete the circle of music."

Rhythm is the number one factor to sounding great as a musician.

WARM UP

Pick a tempo and a gear and play patterns #1, #2, and #3 in both directions. Just think about playing the whole range of a pattern, not a Mode. Each pattern is the same seven notes.

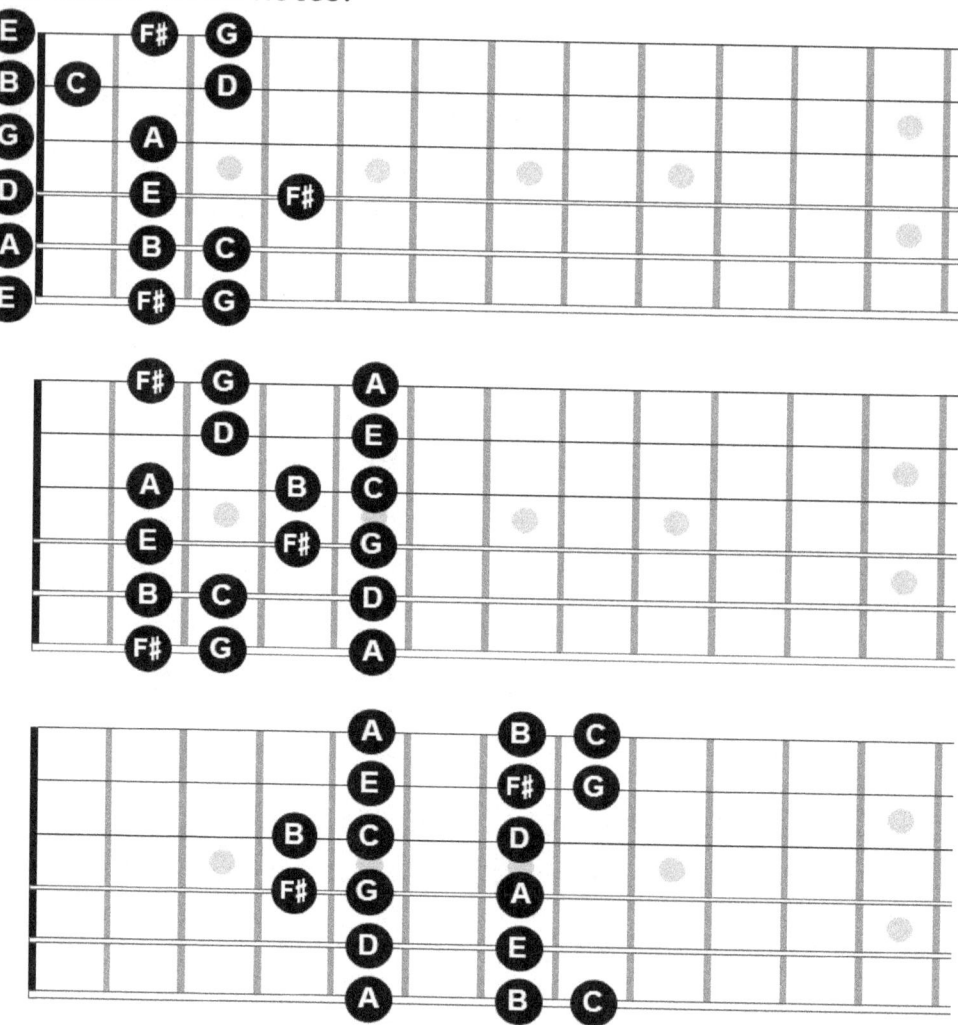

OCTAVE SHAPES

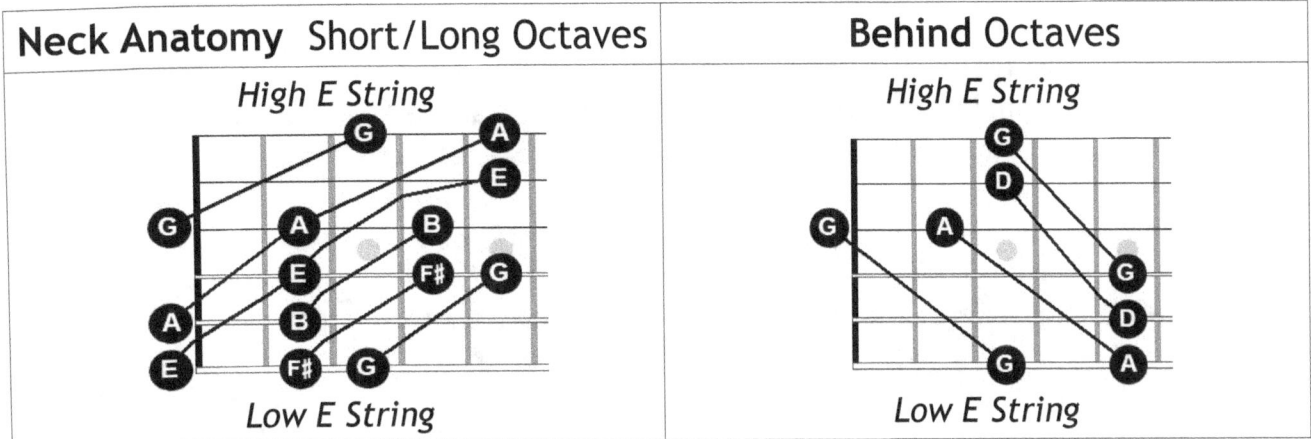

Neck Anatomy Short/Long Octaves	**Behind** Octaves

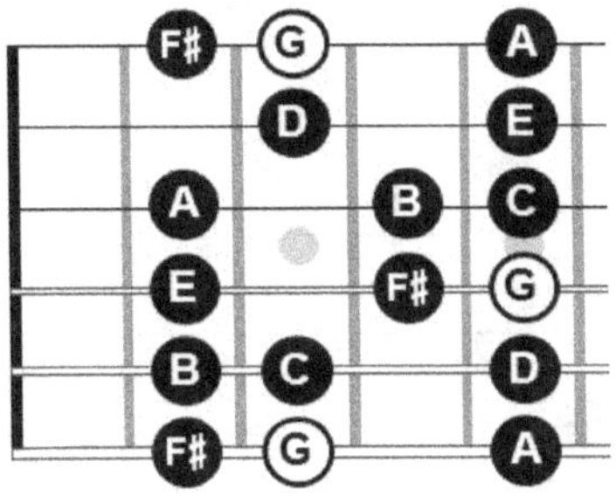

Pattern #2 G Ionian Root *(white)*

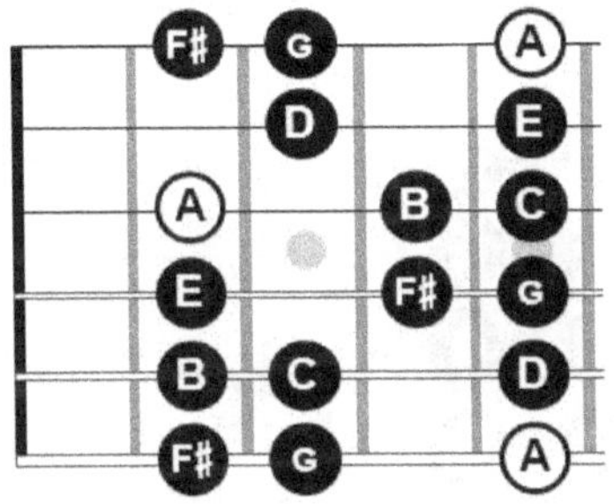

Pattern #2 A Dorian Root *(white)*

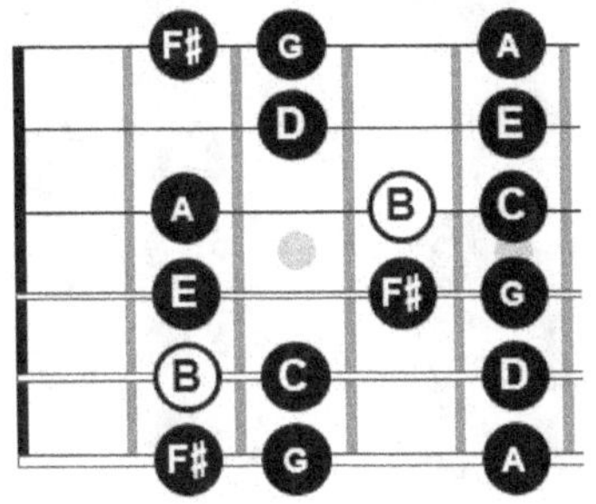

Pattern #2 B Phrygian Root *(white)*

<u>**It's Important to be able to read neck diagrams vertically and horizontally.**</u>

EXERCISE

Play G Ionian, A Dorian, and B Phrygian in EACH Pattern (#1, #2, and #3).
Play the appropriate chord for each Mode (G, Am, or Bm).
Self-gen by alternating one bar chord and one bar scale for 1 octave in 8th notes. Play both octaves when applicable.

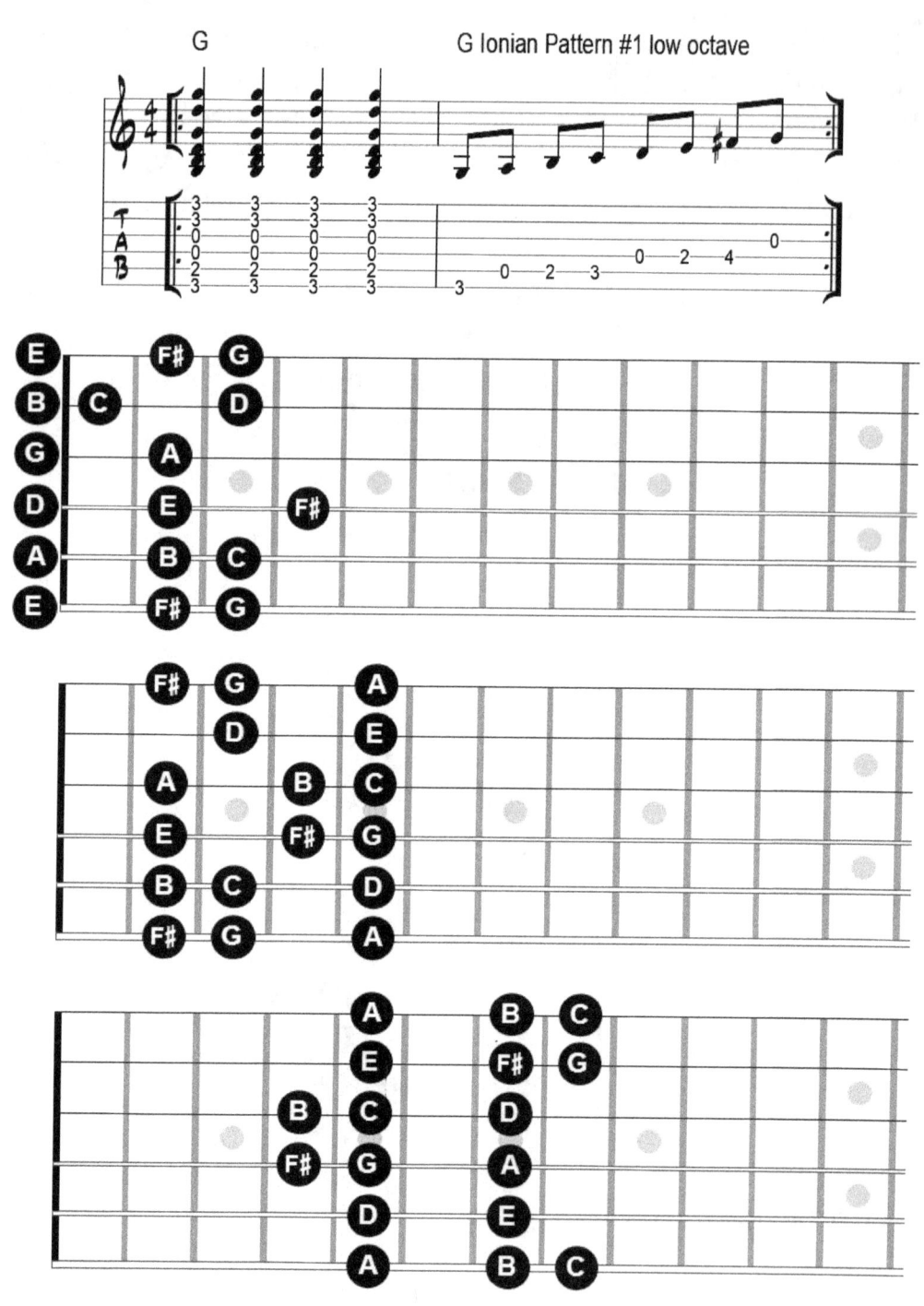

DIATONIC HARMONY REVIEW

I call this chart the world of music on a piece of paper. This is every note of every key, every chord, every scale and mode. This is most likely all the "theory" you will use for the rest of your life. There are things beyond this chart (Harmonic minor, Melodic minor, Full diminished, whole-tone scales and more). But honestly, those extra sounds are usually only a small percentage of what you will use compared to this chart.

	I	ii	iii	IV	V	vi	vii dim
Triads	I Major	ii minor	iii minor	IV Major	V Major	vi minor	vii dim
7th Chords	I Maj7	iim7	iiim7	IV Maj7	V7	vim7	vii-7b5
Modes	Ionian	Dorian	Phrygian	Lydian	Mixolydian	Aeolian	Locrian
DEGREE	TONIC	SUPER TONIC	MEDIANT	SUB DOMINANT	DOMINANT	SUB MEDIANT	LEADING TONE
SOUND	Relative MAJOR*	Happy minor	Dark+Heavy minor	Exotic Major	Funky Major	Relative MINOR*	dark and dim
KEYS 5ths ⬇	C	D	E	F	G	A	B
	G	A	B	C	D	E	F#
	D	E	F#	G	A	B	C#
	A	B	C#	D	E	F#	G#
	E	F#	G#	A	B	C#	D#
	B	C#	D#	E	F#	G#	A#
	Gb/F#	Ab/G#	Bb/A#	Cb/B	Db/C#	Eb/D#	F/E#
	Db	Eb	F	Gb	Ab	Bb	C
	Ab	Bb	C	Db	Eb	F	G
	Eb	F	G	Ab	Bb	C	D
⬆	Bb	C	D	Eb	F	G	A
4ths	F	G	A	Bb	C	D	E

- There are only 3 Major chords and 3 minor chords per Key.
- Any single Major or minor chord can *only* come from one of 3 keys.
- A Major chord can only be either I, IV, or V.
- A minor chord can only be either ii, iii, or vi.
- Don't worry about the diminished chord/mode until you need to (it will be a while).
- For every single song you learn or play you should think about this chart, What is the main chord? What key is it from? What mode is it in?

SONG EXAMPLES BY MODE

Ionian
Imagine *John Lennon*
Don't Stop Believin' *Journey*
No Woman, No Cry *Bob Marley*
Purple Rain *Prince*
Goodbye to Romance *Ozzy Osbourne*
Every Breath You Take *The Police*
Take it Easy *The Eagles*
Let it Be *The Beatles*
Whats Going On *Marvin Gaye*
Jump *Van Halen*
With Or Without You *U2*
Sweet Melissa *The Allman Brothers Band*

Dorian
Moondance *Van Morrison (verse)*
A Horse With No Name *America*
Oye Como Va *Santana*
Breathe *Pink Floyd (verse)*
Down By The River *Neil Young*
Use Me *Bill Withers*
It's Too Late *Carol King (verse)*
Uptown Funk *Bruno Mars*
Light My Fire *(solo) The Doors*

Phrygian
White Rabbit *Jefferson Airplane*
It Was A Very Good Year *Frank Sinatra*
Run Like Hell *Pink Floyd" (verses)*
Black Napkins *Frank Zappa*
Nardis *Miles Davis*
Set the Controls for the Heart of the Sun *Pink Floyd*
Gin and Juice *Snoop Dogg*

Lydian

Over The Hills and Far Away *Led Zeppelin*
Dreams *Fleetwood Mac*
Here Comes My Girl *Tom Petty*
Jane Says *Jane's Addiction*
Inca Roads *Frank Zappa*
Simpsons Theme *Danny Elfman*
Yellow *Coldplay*

Mixolydian

Sympathy For The Devil *The Rolling Stones*
Franklins Tower *The Grateful Dead*
Back in Black *AC/DC*
No Rain *Blind Melon*
On Broadway *George Benson*
Norwegian Wood *George Harrison/The Beatles*
Sweet Child 'O Mine *Guns n Roses*
Sultans of Swing *Dire Straits*
Dream On *Aerosmith*
Sharp Dressed Man *ZZ Top*

Aeolian

All Along the Watchtower *Bob Dylan/Jimi Hendrix*
Layla *(chorus) Eric Clapton*
Eye of the Tiger *Survivor*
Stairway to Heaven *(solo) Led Zeppelin*
Heart of Gold *Neil Young*
Little Wing *Jimi Hendrix*
Comfortably Numb *(verse) Pink Floyd*
The Thrill is Gone *B.B. King*
Smells Like Teen Spirit *Nirvana*
Ain't No Sunshine *Bill Withers*
Zombie *The Cranberries*

Locrian

There are no known songs in Locrian, except rumors of a Bjork song.....

PATTERN vs. MODE

One of the hardest things I had to grapple with as I was learning the guitar and learning about modes was the idea that a pattern was a mode (again, here was music and guitar butting heads). When I was taught the modes at Berklee, it was shown to me as seven different patterns (one for each note/mode). I quickly realized there were only five patterns. Two of them were being used twice.

For example, I was first shown Pattern #2 and was told that it was the Ionian pattern. A few weeks later I was shown the other pattern and it was F# Locrian (the last mode). They are the same. They are Pattern #2.

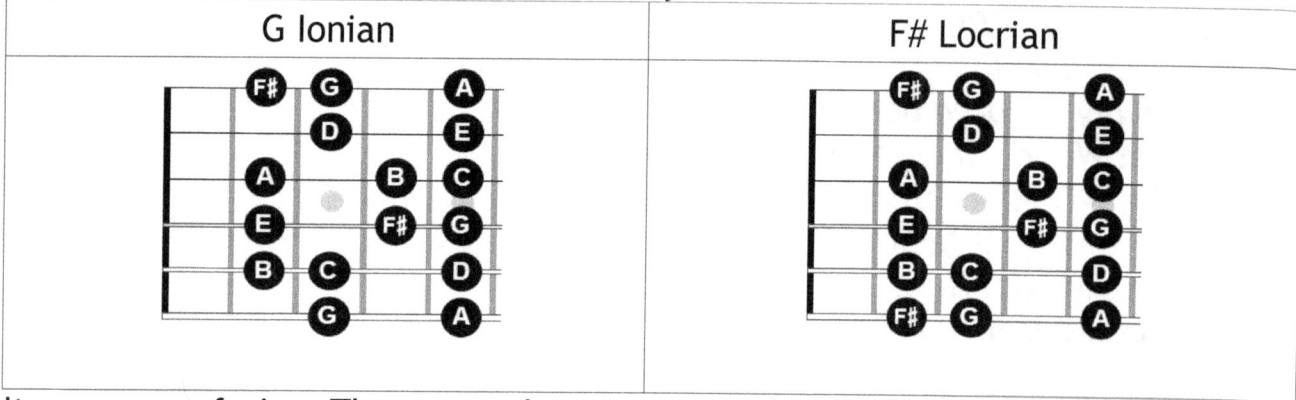

It was so confusing. They were the same pattern but named after the lowest note. It seemed so silly to name a physical shape on your fretboard by a musical job. Imagine if I only played songs in E because that's the lowest note on my instrument. That's absurd. A scale pattern is just a cross section of your instrument with over two octaves worth of notes, **all the notes for that scale**.

This same confusion happens in pentatonics. So often people say pattern #1 is minor (because its lowest note is the Relative minor) and that Pattern #2 is Major (because its lowest note is the Relative Major). That's 50% true, but they are also each other (*they are the same 5 notes*). When people argue about this, it ends quickly when you ask them if #1 is minor and #2 is Major, then what are Pattern #3, #4 or #5 called?

Just think. If you knew all of the notes of all chords, scales and keys as a musician, AND you could quickly see all of the notes on your fretboard, you would not need scale patterns anymore! How freeing is that? Now think about the fact that in each of the 5 mode patterns there are about 20 notes per pattern. Multiply this by 5 patterns and you are learning over 100 locations of dots on the fretboard to help you remember where 7 notes are! My mind was blown when I realized this, and learning the notes seemed even more rewarding and less intimidating than I thought. *The key to learning the notes on the fretboard was octaves*!

- Each pattern (Pentatonic or Mode) is 2 octaves.
- Guitar is 3 usable octaves. (4 octaves in E if you bend the highest note)
- Every pattern is all the modes. Its all seven notes. (*IMPORANT*)
- Often the lowest note of the pattern is not the name of the scale.
- Any pattern is just a cross section of two octaves of the same seven notes.

Root position pattern vs numbered patterns

I made a choice a long time ago to always try to be musical first and a guitar player second. Once I realized the mode patterns were the same seven notes and there were only actually five patterns I decided to just number them, one through five. I would then see them as a key and find the root note of the mode. As I grew as a musician and was touring full time, playing shows five nights a week the patterns started to dissolve. I just started seeing the whole neck light up with what ever notes I needed. It's a very freeing feeling.

In learning patterns you will definitely see and hear people talk about the Ionian pattern and the Dorian pattern. They are referring to patterns #1 and #2 respectfully. The term ROOT POSITION means that the scale pattern's lowest note is the ROOT of that mode. It can be a quick reference when locating a Mode pattern on the fretboard. BUT It can be very restrictive if you don't fully understand that each pattern of the key is the same set of notes. Its how you use it as a musician.

ROOT POSITION NAMES
Pattern #1 - Aeolian
Pattern #2 - Ionian/Locrian
Pattern #3 - Dorian
Pattern #4 - Phrygian/Lydian
Pattern #5 - Mixolydian

You must realize that
ALL FIVE PATTERNS ARE THE SAME SEVEN NOTES IN ANY GIVEN KEY.

LYDIAN

Lydian is the fourth degree of a major scale. It is a Major mode built on a Major chord, the IV chord. Lydian is the second Major mode after Ionian. Remember, the chords and the scale make the mode. In the key of G we have G A B C D E F# G. If we start and resolve to the C note we will have C Lydian.

C D E F# G A B C

CHORD PROGRESSION			CHORD RELATIONSHIP - *AS IS*
			CHORD RELATIONSHIP - *TRADITIONAL* *
C	D		IV V
			I II*
C	G D		IV I V
			I V II*
C	D G		IV V I
			I II V*
C	Em D		IV vi V
			I iii II*

Lydian is the second Major mode after Ionian. It has the lighthearted quality that Ionian has but it has a dreamy exotic sound. Even though it's major, there is a mystical quality to it. Guitar players love to solo in it, ask Satriani or Vai (he would say ask Frank). Lydian is often substituted for the Ionian scale as a chord scale in jazz.

If you look at the "traditional" chord relationship you will see there are no IV chords. Lydian's quirkiness comes from the fact that there is no note a Perfect 4th above it, meaning there is no IV chord. This makes chord progressions more difficult to make sound like Lydian.

PRACTICE

In each pattern play a C Lydian scale ascending and descending.

Play first as quarter-notes and then as eighth-notes.

Self-Gen by playing 1 bar of a C Major chord and 1 bar of scale in 8th notes.

Play both octaves in Pattern #3

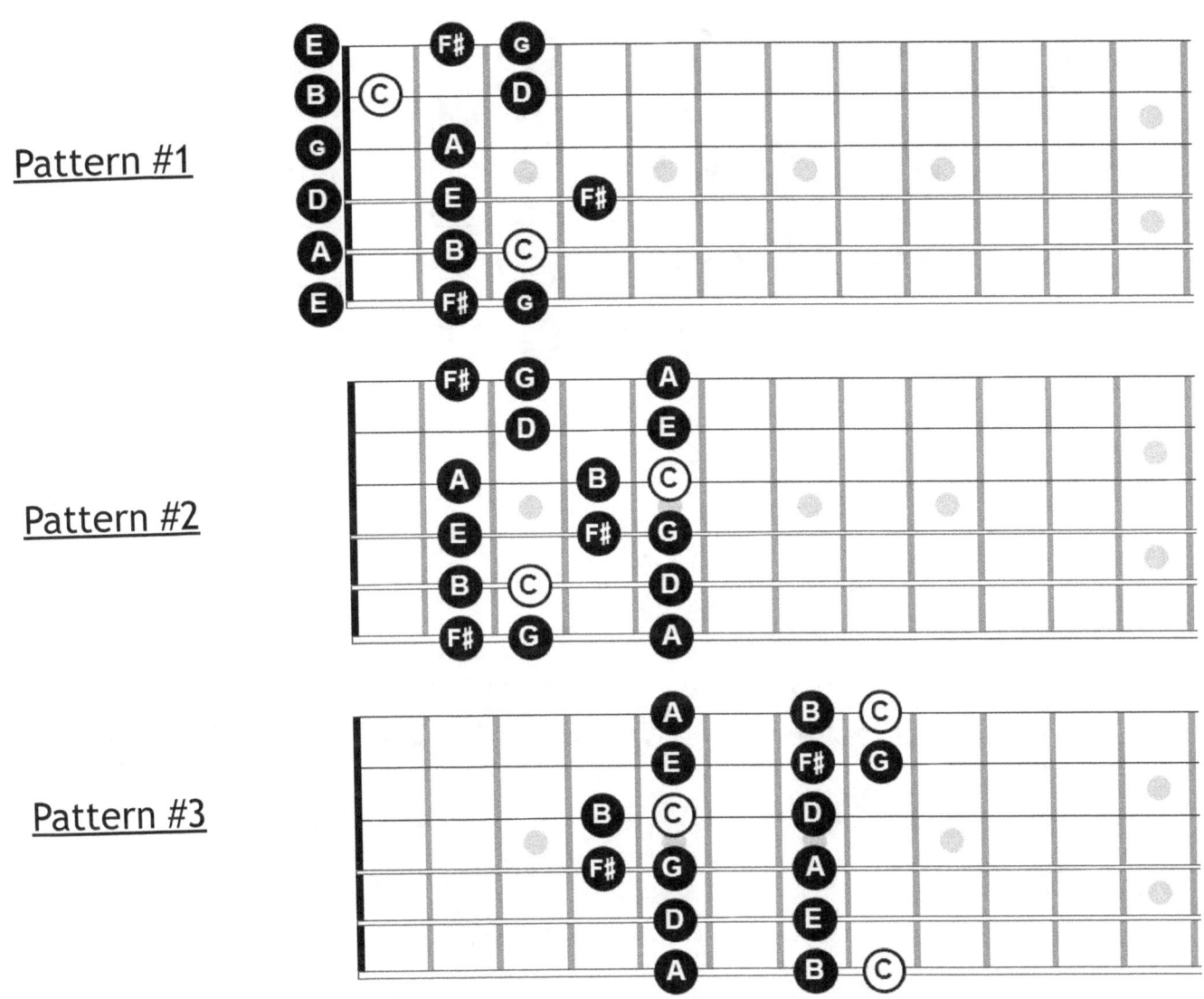

Pattern #1

Pattern #2

Pattern #3

BACKING TRACKS

All patterns for all modes (so far, three patterns, four modes)

G= Root of G Ionian

A= Root of A Dorian

B= Root of B Phrygian

C= Root of C Lydian

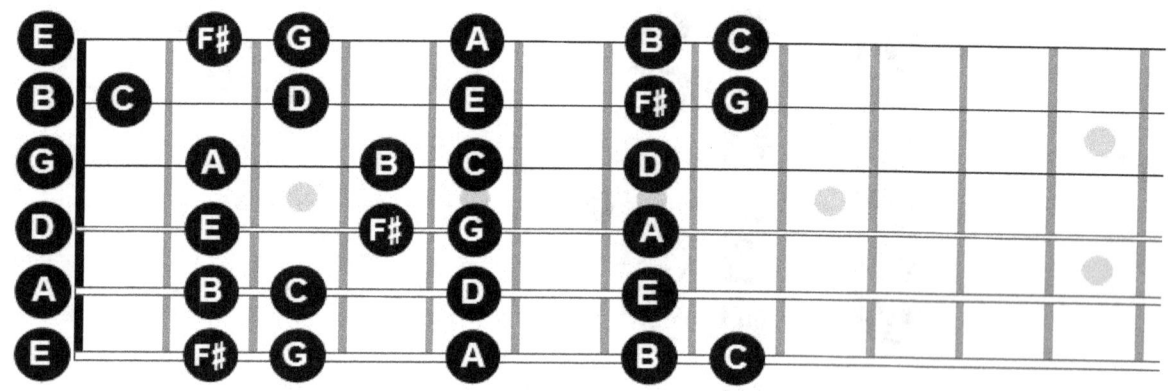

Pattern #1

Pattern #2

Pattern #3

BACKING TRACKS
PLAY ALONG

www.LeadGuitarWorkshop.com

G Ionian

|G |D |Em |C |

A Dorian

|Am |D |

B Phrygian

|Bm |C |

C Lydian

|C |D |

SUMMARY

We are musicians. We are guitar players.
We learn the language of music. Melody, Harmony, and Rhythm
We learn the craft of playing the guitar as an instrument.

MODES are a function of a scale. You can start any scale on any one of its own notes.

The MODES are: **Ionian, Dorian, Phrygian, Lydian, Mixolydian, Aeolian, Locrian.**

MODES are CHORD PROGRESSIONS. You can use any of the chords in a key to be the "main" chord, the TONIC.

We learn to see common modal chord progressions.

Diatonic Harmony = **I ii iii IV V vi vii°**

As guitar players it is extremely helpful to see your octaves.

We learned how to add two notes (C and F#) to our scale pattern by filling in the pentatonic pattern #1 and pattern #2.

You will use Pattern #1, #2 and #3 for ALL 12 Keys, one for each fret. The three patterns are always connected and in the same order, always.

Don't forget that at the 12th fret the guitar (an music world) starts over again an octave higher.

We use BACKING TRACKS and SELF GENERATE to give a real time context to our playing.

ALL 5 PATTERNS SOUND THE SAME. THEY ARE THE SAME SEVEN NOTES IN ANY GIVEN KEY. They help you use your whole fretboard.

CHAPTER 5

TUNE IN

"I am a musician and a guitar player. Music is my language and my guitar is my voice. Music is Melody, Harmony and Rhythm. I develop my language skills and my instrument skills. They are two separate worlds working together to complete the circle of music."

Rhythm is the number one factor to sounding great as a musician.

WARM UP

Pick a tempo and a gear and play patterns #1, #2, and #3 in both directions. Just think about playing the whole range of a pattern, not a Mode. Each pattern is the same seven notes.

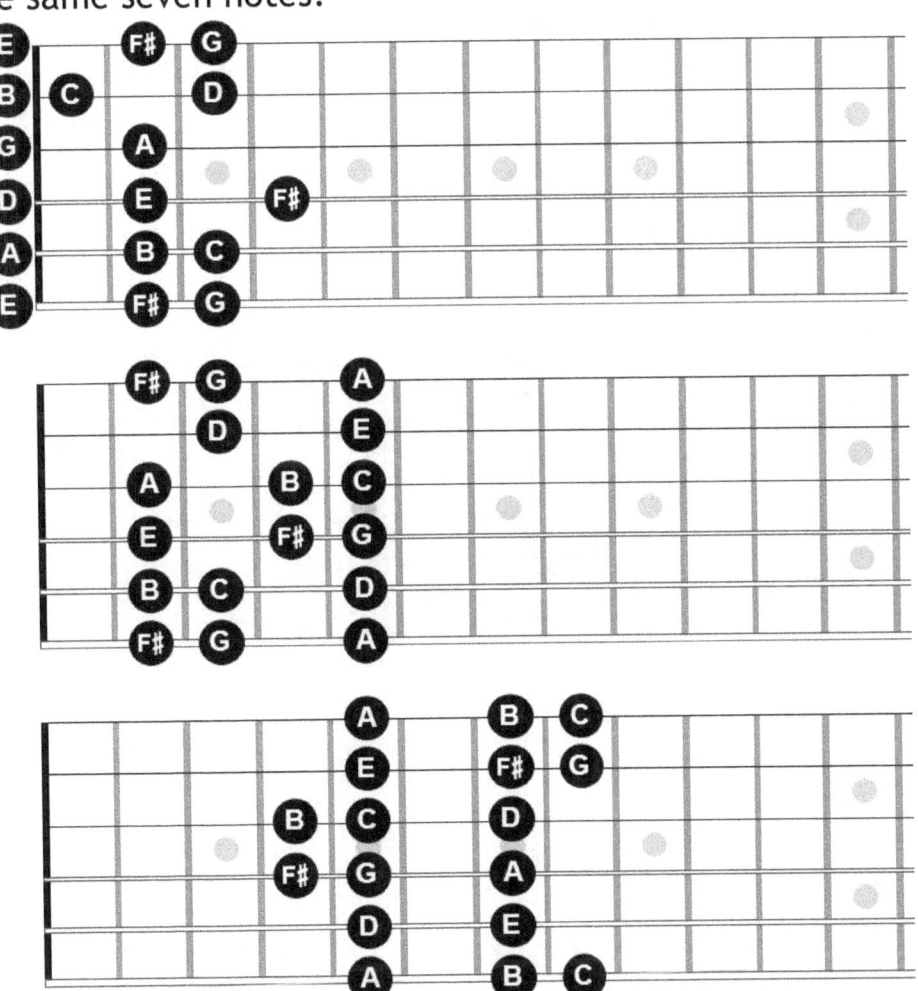

EXERCISE

- Choose G Ionian, A Dorian, B Phrygian, or C Lydian.
- Self-Gen with one bar of the chord and one bar of 1 octave scale in 8th notes.
- Do the same mode in each of the three patterns.

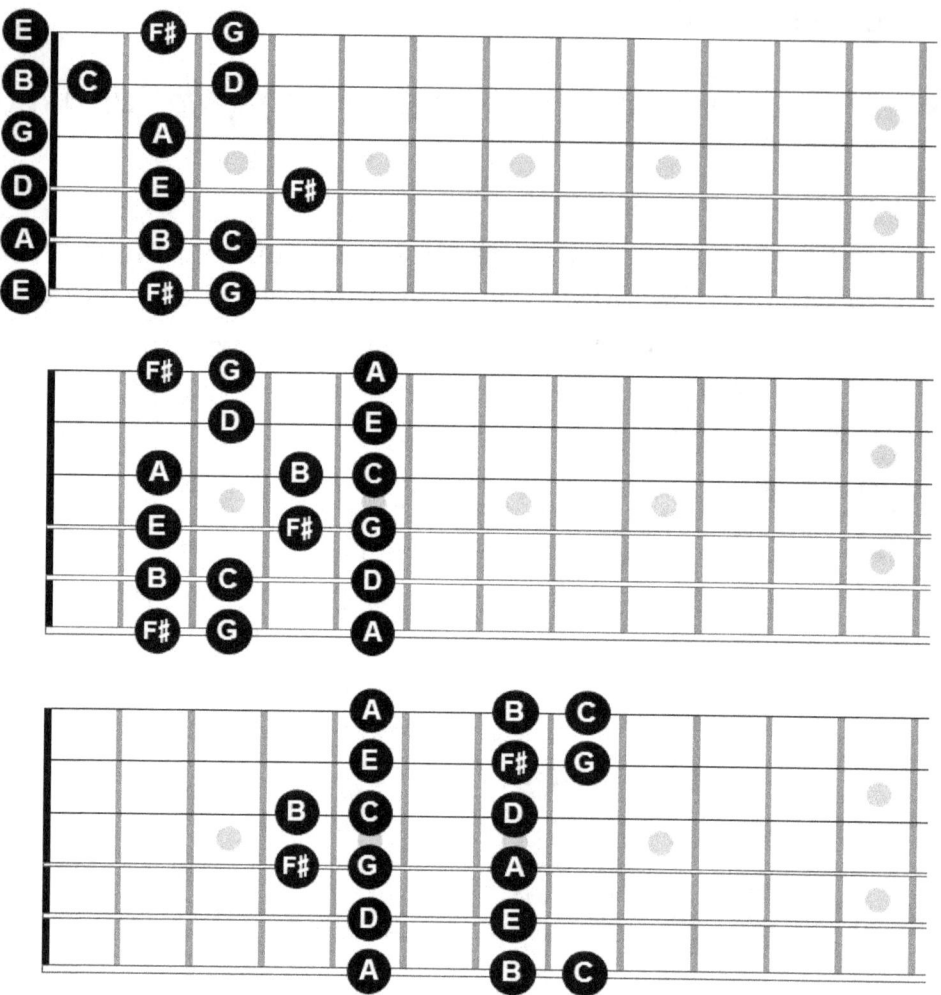

EXERCISE (cont.)

Any mode in any pattern.

Here are 4 examples. Ascend and descend the scale.

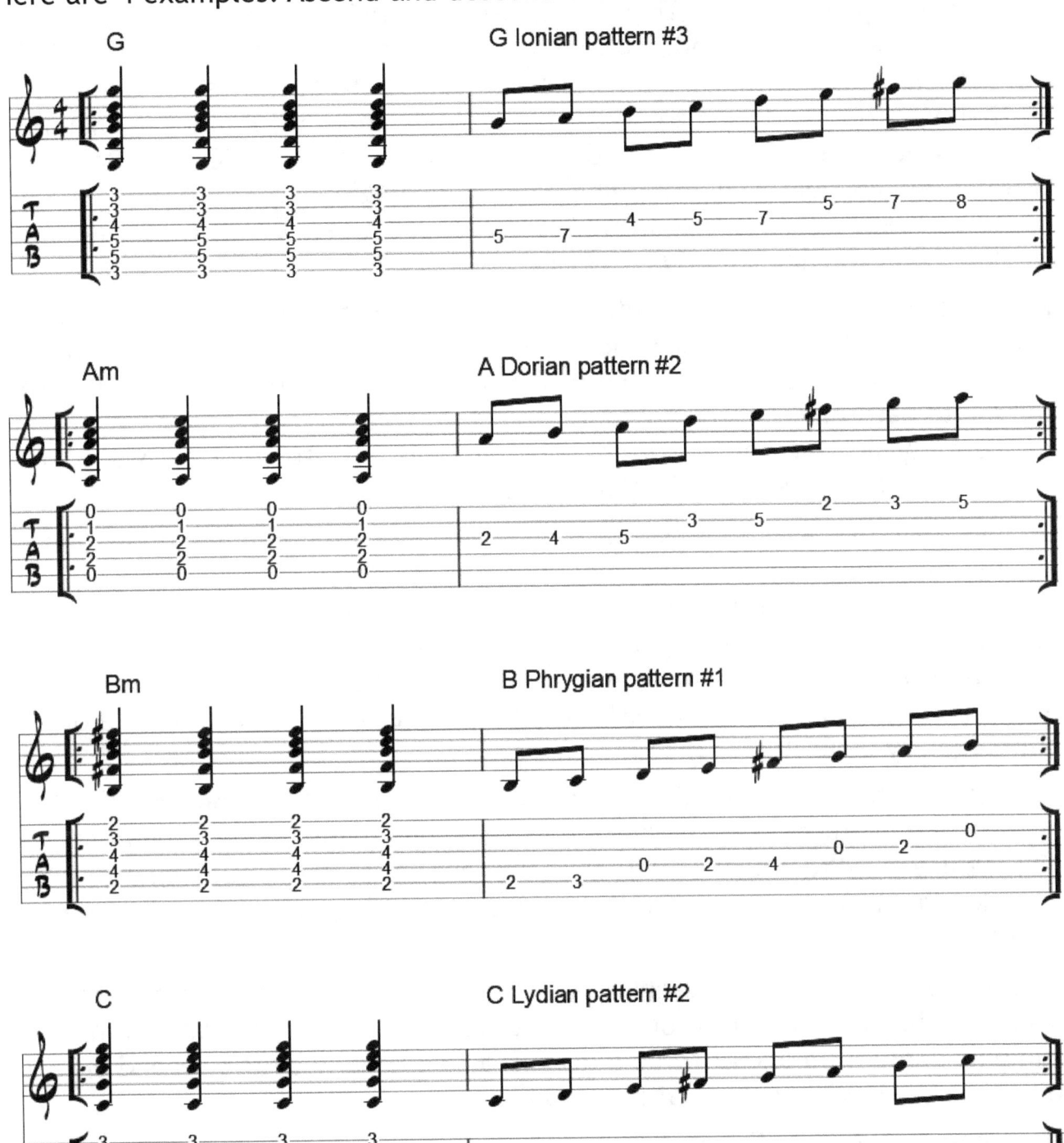

REVIEW

As musicians we've talked about how we see modes in action as **melodies** and as **chord progressions**. They are a cause and effect of each other. If I start singing a D note and add more notes to find a scale made up of D E F# G A B C, then I would be singing a D Mixolydian scale (from the key of G Ionian). If I then wanted to add some chords, the D Major chord would be the "Main" chord. I would then find the the other chords in the key of G (G, Am, Bm, C, Em) that would work well with the melody I am singing. My chord progression would be based on a D chord, using the chords from the key of G. I would be playing a D Mixolydian chord progression.

This order could also be reversed. You may start strumming some chords and find yourself playing a D chord and a C and G after. You are strumming a D Mixolydian chord progression. If you then started singing (or someone else) the ear would naturally find the notes in the Key of G. It would be hard to accidentally sing the Key of D Major. That key has C# note. Your ear would not let you sing that note, especially over the C chord.

Even as scale or chord progressions the Modes have a sound and mood. To me, Ionian sounds like vanilla. I love vanilla, but it's vanilla. Dorian is the Happy minor. There is a bit of hope in Dorian. It makes you crack a smile. Phrygian is strong, dark and heavy, falling somewhere between Flamenco and metal. Phrygian is a powerful sound, definitely the darkest and heaviest. Lydian is the exotic major, kind of dream like. It is Major but has a twist to it, a little off but elegantly beautiful.

The diatonic formula created by stacking every other note in the Major scale gives us the qualities of each chord in the key, one named after each note. All 12 keys are created equal. The formula can answer so many questions about what key or Mode you are in, and when you change keys or have a borrowed chord.

Memorizing the formula is essential and being able to retro fit chords into it is also important. It's a process of elimination. Any one chord, Major or minor, can only come from one of three places in a key. Usually by the second or third chord you will know what key you are in.

Our Diatonic Harmony Formula:

REVIEW CONTINUED

As guitar players we map out patterns across our fretboard to highlight the notes that are in the key of G. The resulting notes form the G Ionian scale and all of its modes including A Dorian, B Phrygian, C Lydian, D Mixolydian, E Aeolian, and F# Locrian.

So far we have filled in four of the five patterns that connect the 12 frets of our fretboard. There is a lot of confusion over the naming and use of patterns for guitar players. Always keep yourself in musical check. What are you trying to do musically?

I believe the easiest way to learn the modes as patterns is to fill in the pentatonic shapes you already know. The Modes have two half steps. You are literally adding two notes to make a pentatonic into a seven note scale. Those two notes add the "color" or sounds of the modes.

We start by filling the pentatonic patterns for the Key we are in. Then we are able to see all of its modes.

We talked previously about ROOT POSITION pattern names. It is so often taught that there are seven patterns, one each starting on a note of the scale. That is 1/7 true. Each pattern is the same seven notes for two full octaves. It is extremely limiting and destructive to think of a pattern as just one musical scale when it is actually seven. In fact if you look at any of the patterns they each have two or usually three notes on the low E string. Why is just the lowest sounding one the ROOT and not the one right above it? It never made sense to me. I felt duped when I learned the the seven mode patterns I learned from scratch were the five pentatonics I already knew (plus two notes).

When you, as a musician, decide to play pentatonics as a sound, you will play the pentatonic of the chord itself just like you always did. For example if you are in A Dorian, and you are on the 5th fret, you are in Mode pattern #3 (Pentatonic pattern #3 for the Key of G, which contains A Dorian). BUT if you decided you didn't want the extra color a mode provides you would simple revert back to an A minor pentatonic. That would put pattern #1 on the 5th fret.

PATTERN #4

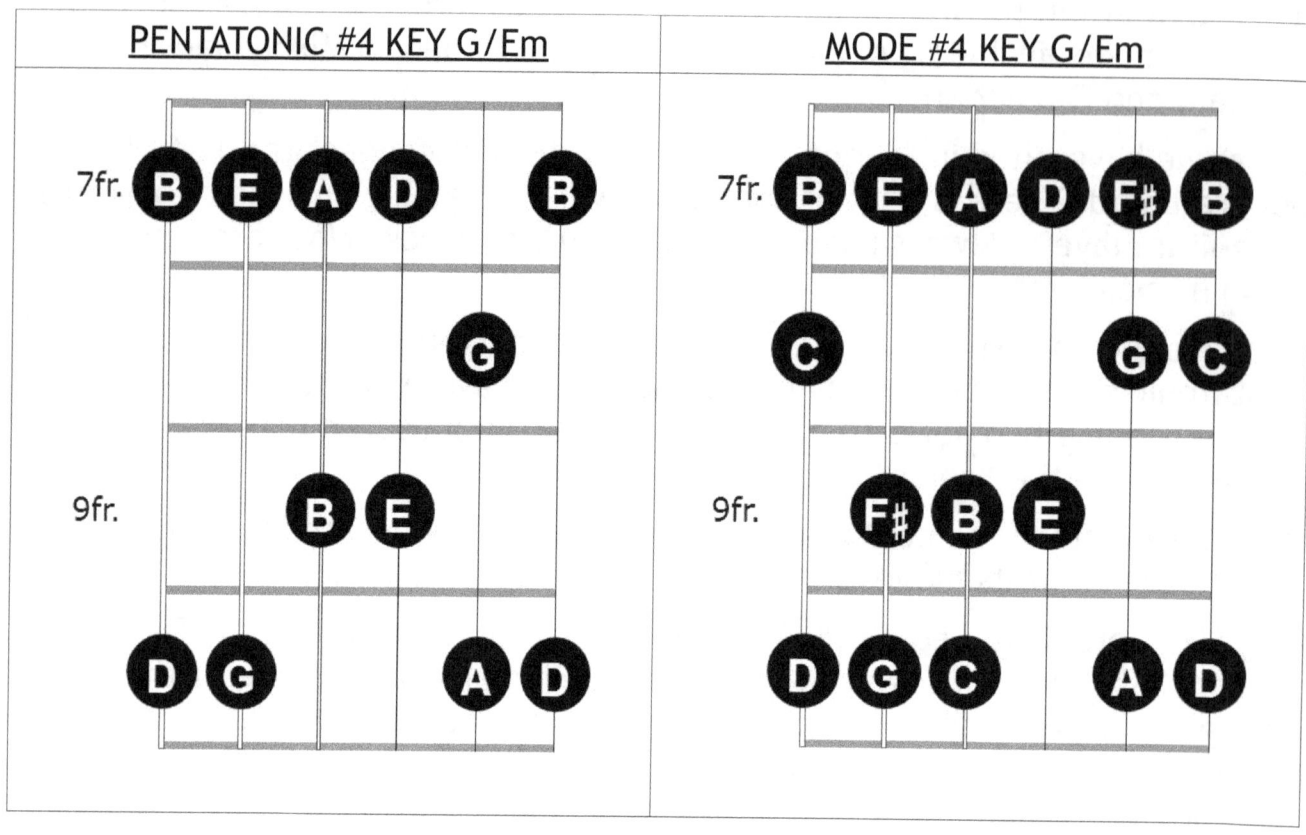

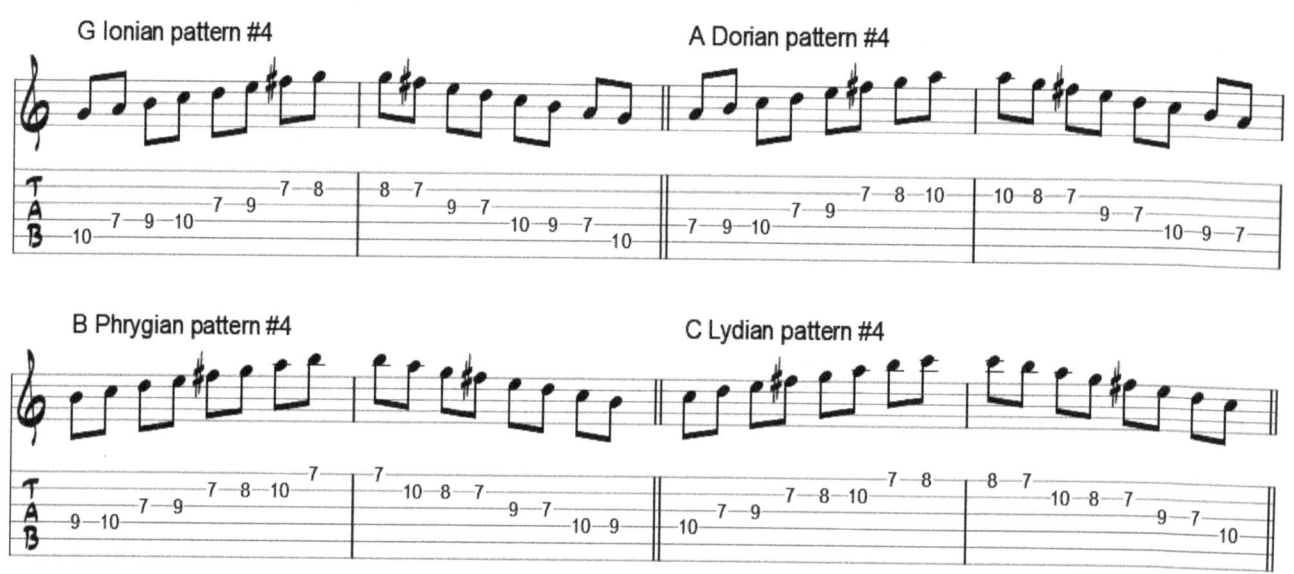

MIXOLYDIAN

Mixolydian or "Mixo" for short is the third Major mode in a key and is built off of the V chord in the key. Mixolydian is almost as common as Ionian. I like to call it the "funky Major." It has a strong and proud sound compared to the softer Ionian sound and the exotic sound of Lydian.

CHORD PROGRESSION	CHORD RELATIONSHIP - *AS IS* CHORD RELATIONSHIP - *TRADITIONAL**
|D |C |	V IV I bVII*
|D |C G |	V IV I I bVII IV*
|D C |G D |	V IV I V I bVII IV I*
|D G |Am G |	V I ii I I IV v IV*

*Traditional notation requires you start the numbering on the "main" chord and then adjust the intervals accordingly. **D** is now the "one" chord and the **C** is a Whole step below, so it's considered a flat seven away. It's complicated.

PRACTICE

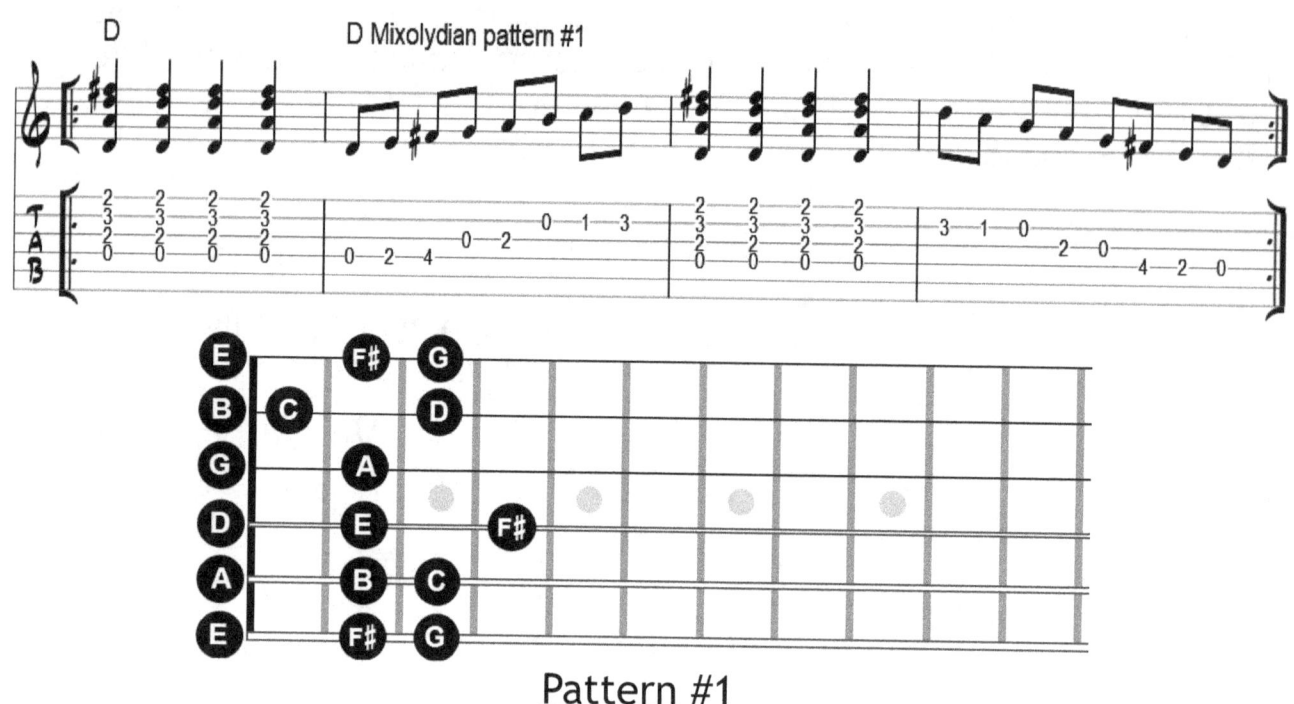

Pattern #1

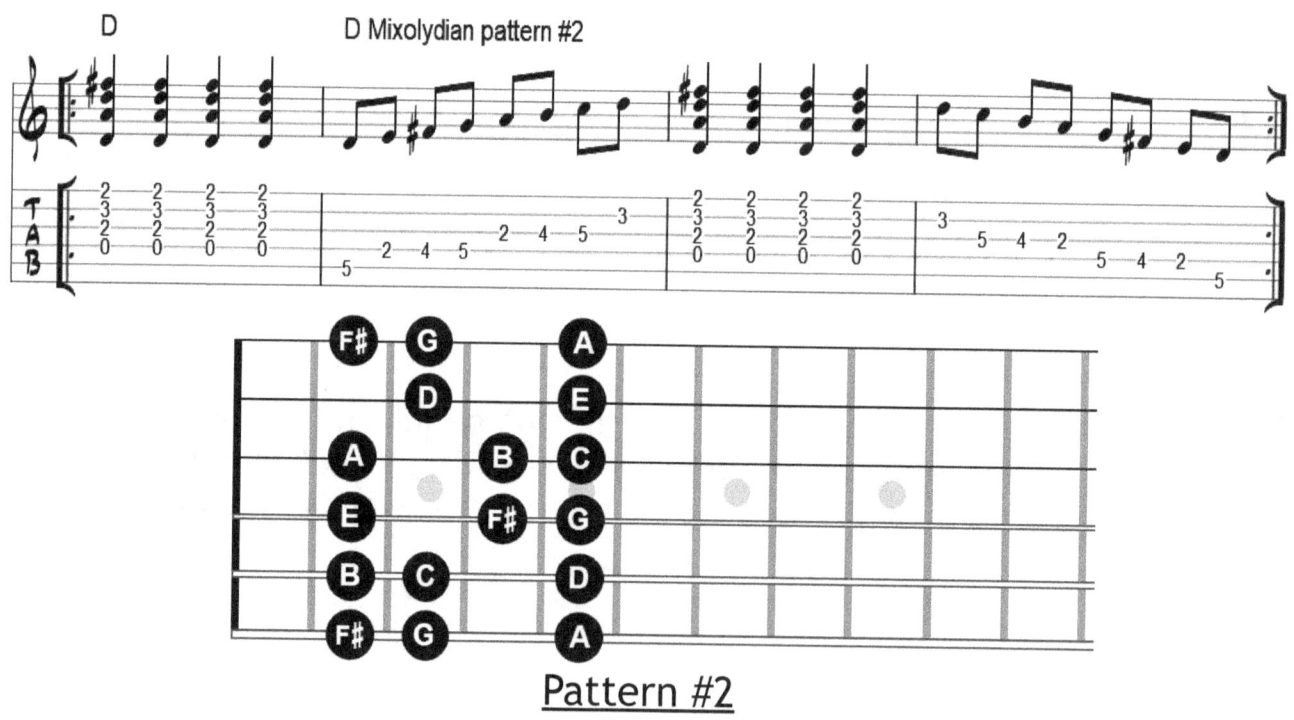

Pattern #2

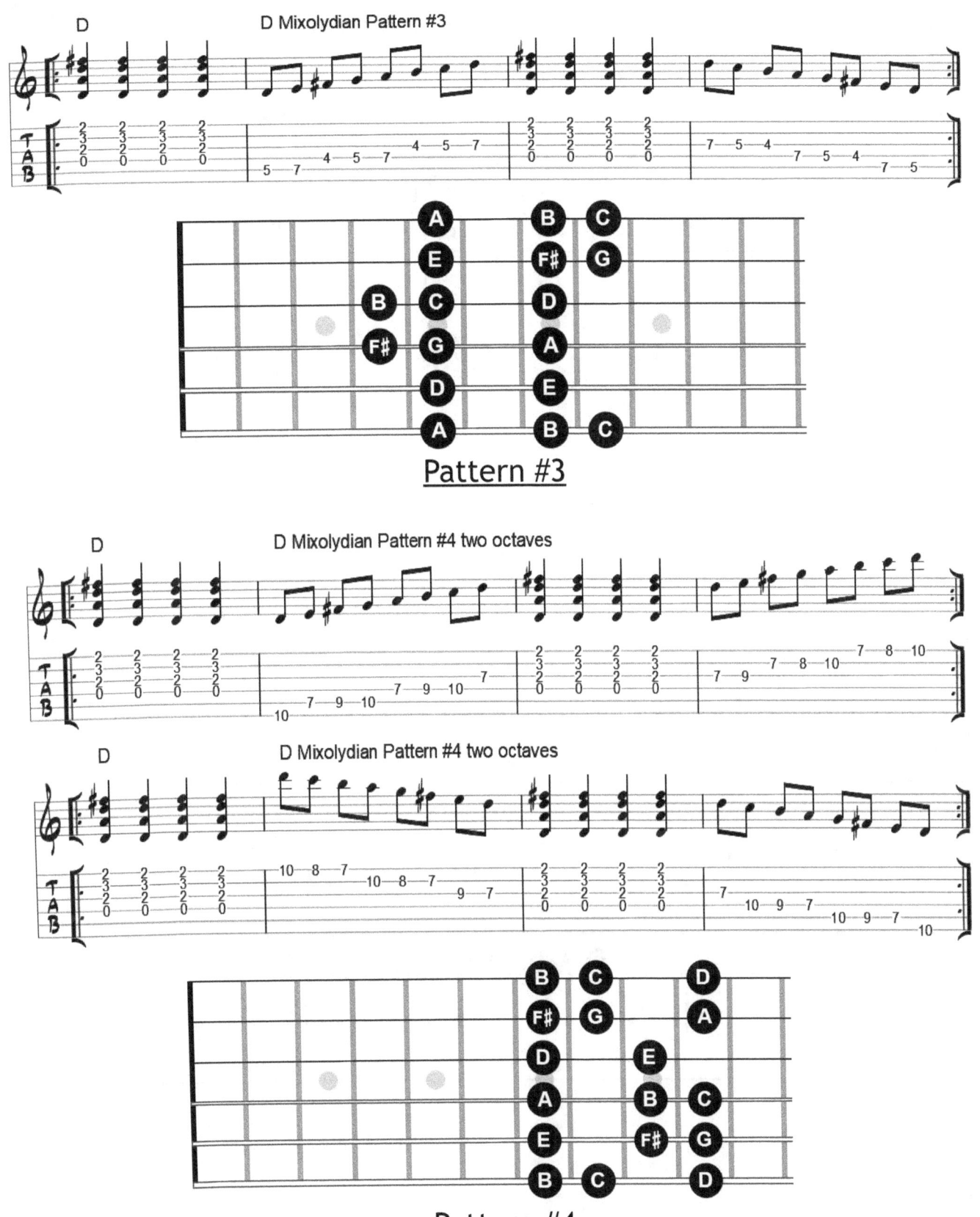

Pattern #3

Pattern #4

BACKING TRACKS

BACKING TRACKS
<u>PLAY ALONG</u>
www.LeadGuitarWorkshop.com

G Ionian				
|G	|D	|Em	|C	|

A Dorian		
| Am	|D	|

B Phrygian		
|Bm	|C	|

C Lydian		
|C	|D	|

D Mixolydian				
|D	|C	|G	|D	|

All FOUR Patterns in Key of G. They are all the same 7 notes. They are all the modes.

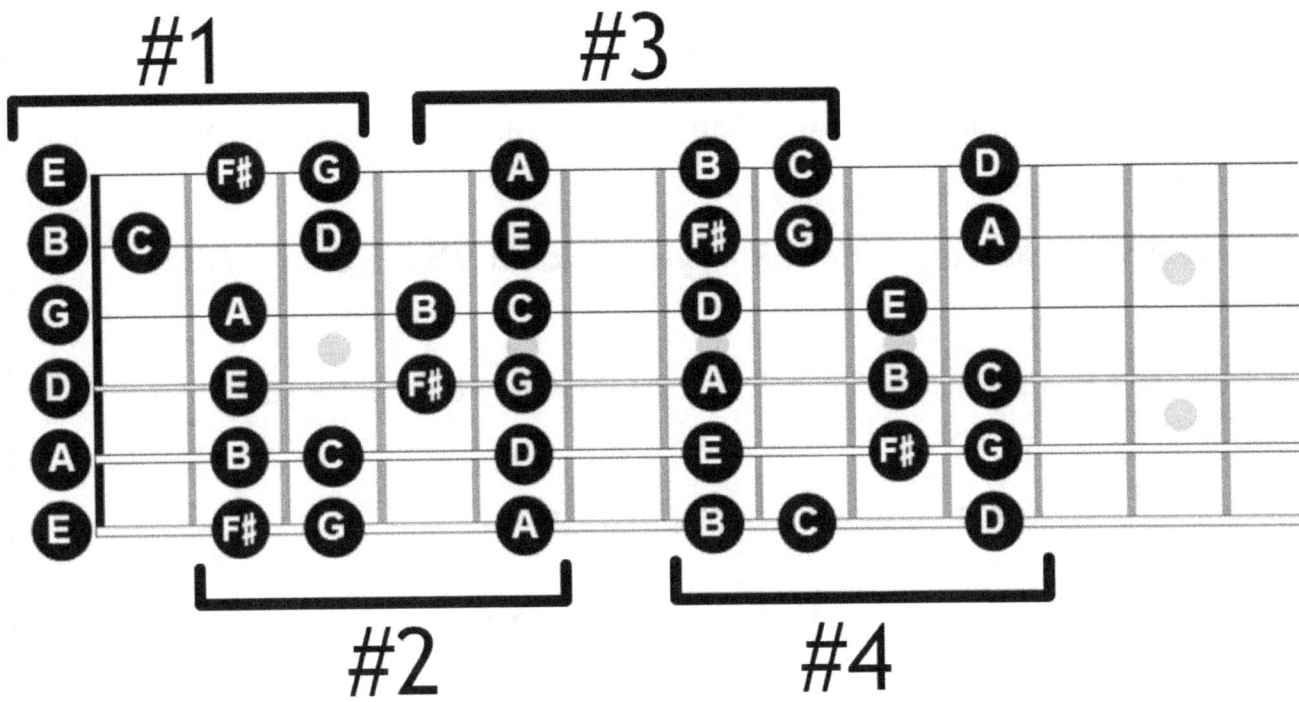

The Lick (D Mixo)

Extra Licks

SUMMARY

We are musicians. We are guitar players.
We learn the language of music. Melody, Harmony, and Rhythm
We learn the craft of playing the guitar as an instrument.

MODES are a function of a SCALE. You can start any scale on any one of its own notes.

The MODES are: **Ionian, Dorian, Phrygian, Lydian, Mixolydian, Aeolian, Locrian.**

MODES are CHORD PROGRESSIONS. You can use any of the chords in a key to be the "main" chord, the TONIC.

We learn to see common modal chord progressions.

Diatonic Harmony = **I ii iii IV V vi vii°**

As guitar players it is extremely helpful to see your octaves.

You will use Pattern #1, #2, #3 and #4 for ALL 12 Keys, one for each fret. The three patterns are always connected and in the same order, always.

Don't forget that at the 12th fret the guitar (an music world) starts over again an octave higher.

We use BACKING TRACKS and SELF GENERATE to give a real time context to our playing.

ALL 5 PATTERNS SOUNDS THE SAME. THEY ARE THE SAME SEVEN NOTES IN ANY GIVEN KEY. They help you use your whole fretboard.

CHAPTER 6

TUNE IN

"I am a musician and a guitar player. Music is my language and my guitar is my voice. Music is Melody, Harmony and Rhythm. I develop my language skills and my instrument skills. They are two separate worlds working together to complete the circle of music."

Rhythm is the number one factor to sounding great as a musician.

WARM UP

The 4 patterns   Play in time   full pattern ascend and descend.

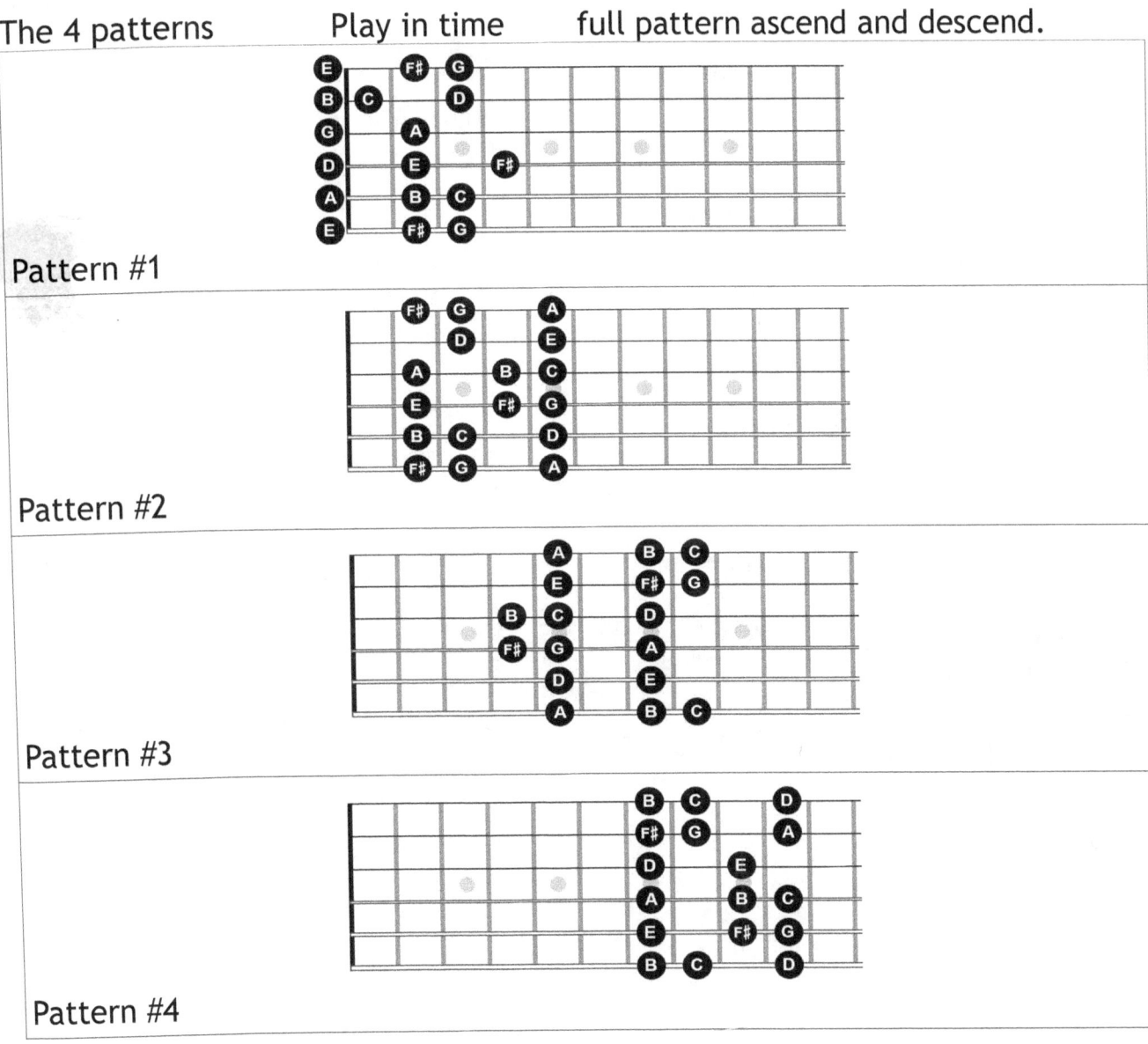

Pattern #1

Pattern #2

Pattern #3

Pattern #4

EXERCISE

Play G Ionian, A Dorian, B Phrygian, C Lydian and D Mixolydian in Pattern #4.
Self generate with one bar chord and one bar scale.

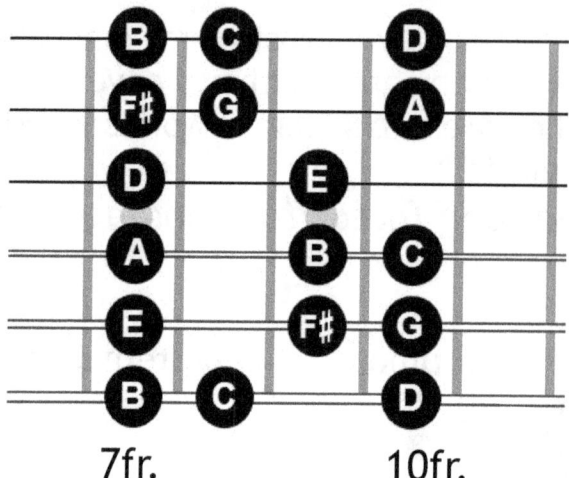

7fr.   10fr.

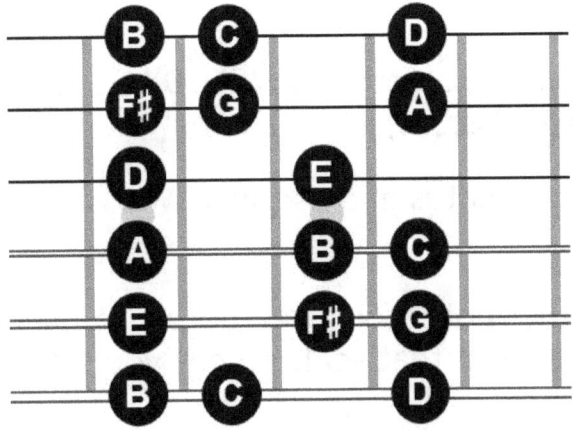

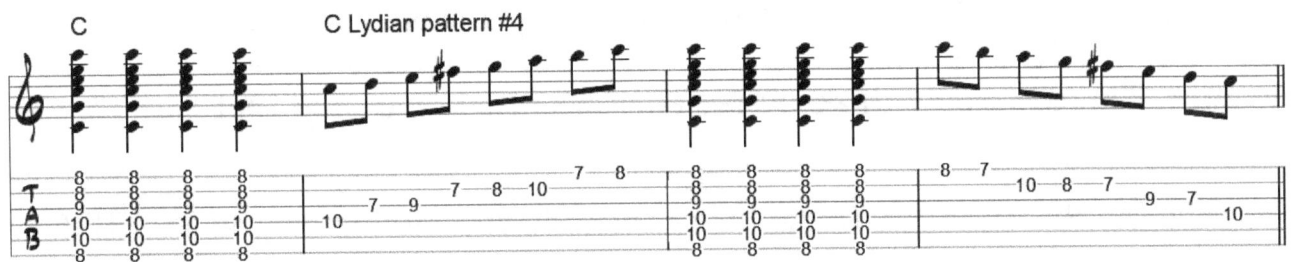

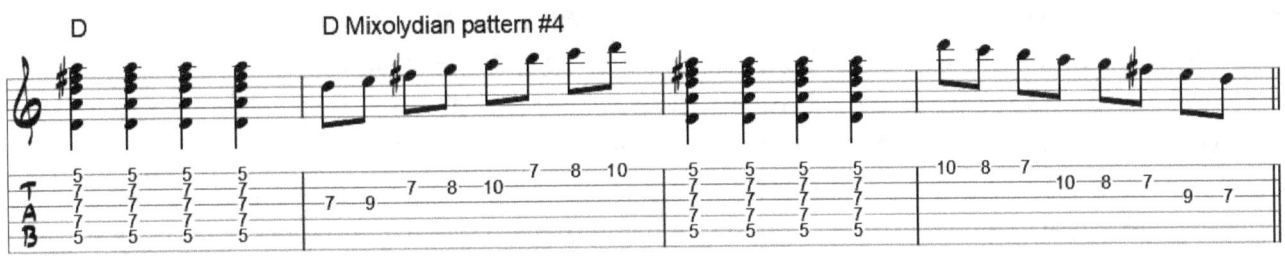

REVIEW

As Musicians we are looking at modes as MELODY (as scale ideas), and as HARMONY (as chord progressions).

You can take any of the 12 notes and use WWHWWWH to make a MAJOR (IONIAN) scale.

You then stack every other note, for three notes, to make a TRIAD. You do this for each of the seven notes in that scale to get you seven TRIADS with the same note name.

The resulting formula is the Diatonic Formula. **I ii iii IV V vi vii**dim

Any one of those NOTES or CHORDS can be the "main" one. From there MODES happen.

Always do your musical thinking first and then go to your instrument. Ask yourself, "What is the main chord?" "What is the main note?" "What key am I in?" "What mode am I in?" Once you have answered those questions then you can go to your instrument.

Remember when looking at a chord progression, any one chord can ONLY come from 3 of the 12 keys. There are only three places a MAJOR chord lives, the I, IV and V. There are only three places a MINOR chord lives and that is the ii, iii, and the vi.

Ionian is the RELATIVE MAJOR and (soon we will see) Aeolian is the RELATIVE MINOR.

As a guitar player we need help to remember where those seven notes of a key are on our fretboard. So we have patterns, and seemingly a ton of them, depending on how you look at it. There are more methods than I can imagine on how to do this and they all seem like a bird tufting its feathers to impress you or intimidate you. There are only seven notes in the scale you are looking at. They are the same seven notes in each of the seven modes that uses them. There is NO need to renumber patterns to illustrate this. There are only FIVE patterns on your fretboard. As a musician those five patterns will have SEVEN sounds in them.

ALL FIVE PATTERNS HAVE THE SAME SEVEN NOTES AND SOUND EXACTLY THE SAME (depending on what mode you are in).

PATTERN #5

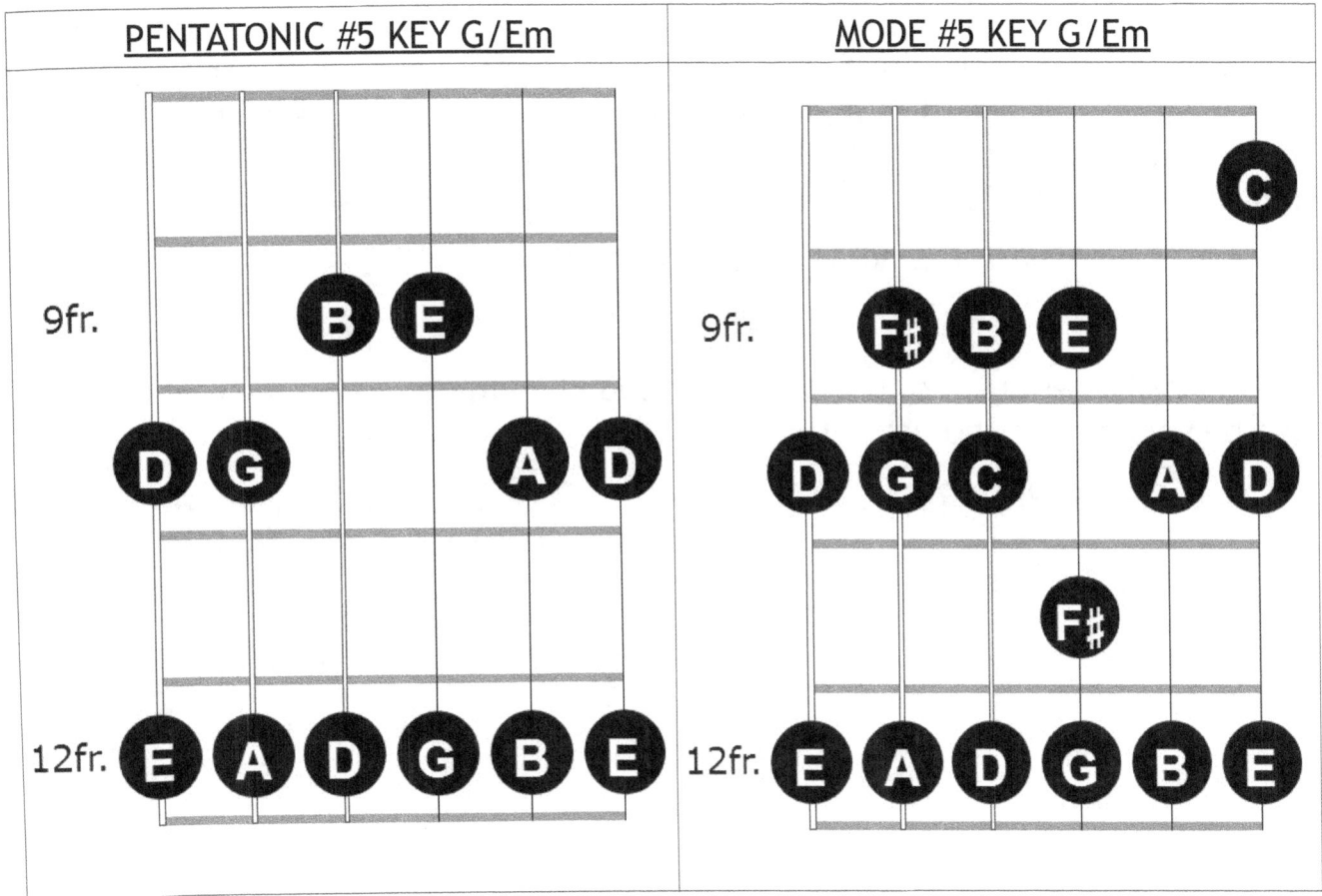

| PENTATONIC #5 KEY G/Em | MODE #5 KEY G/Em |

REMEMBER: We are filling in the five patterns of the Key of G/Em. We are making the pentatonic into a seven note scale (by adding F# and C). This will give us patterns of the notes of G Major, and thus, all of its Modes too.

When you are in pentatonics you usually match the pentatonic to the chord and not the key. But you can find examples of playing in the key, like "Sweet Home Alabama" where the main chord is a D chord (DCG). The chords are from the Key of G and it is a D mixolydian song. But the soloist chose to play a G Major pentatonic (from the key, not the chord). You will hear people get very confused when they look at it as if he is in E minor pentatonic (the relative).

AEOLIAN

If Ionian is "THE" Major, then Aeolian is "THE" minor. It is the Relative minor to Ionian. Aeolian is the start of the minor keys and is known as "The Natural minor." Aeolian is the third minor mode and it is based off the vi chord in a key. Aeolian is very serious. I call it the "no funny business" minor. It's sad and somber but can be Epic as well.

In our key of G Major the notes of E Aeolian are:

E F# G A B C D

Aeolian is the serious, no funny business sounding minor. Sad and stoic, it can also be very strong and powerful.

CHORD PROGRESSION					CHORD RELATIONSHIP - *AS IS* CHORD RELATIONSHIP - *TRADITIONAL**
|Em	|D	|C	|D	|	vi V IV V i *b*VII *b*VI *b*VII*

|Em	|D	|C	|Am	|	vi V IV ii i *b*VII *b*VI iv*
|Em	|D	|Am	|C	|	vi V ii IV i *b*VII iv *b*VI*
|Em	|Am	|Bm	|Am	|	vi ii iii vi i iv v iv*
|Em	|C	|D	|Em	|	vi IV V vi i *b*VI *b*VII vi*
|Em	|C	|D	|G	|	vi IV V I i *b*VI *b*VII *b*III*

Traditional notation requires you start the numbering on the "main" chord and then adjust the intervals accordingly. **Em** becomes the "one" chord and the **D** is a Whole step below, so its considered a flat seven away. It's complicated.

PRACTICE

Practice pattern #5 as pattern practice, not thinking music modes.

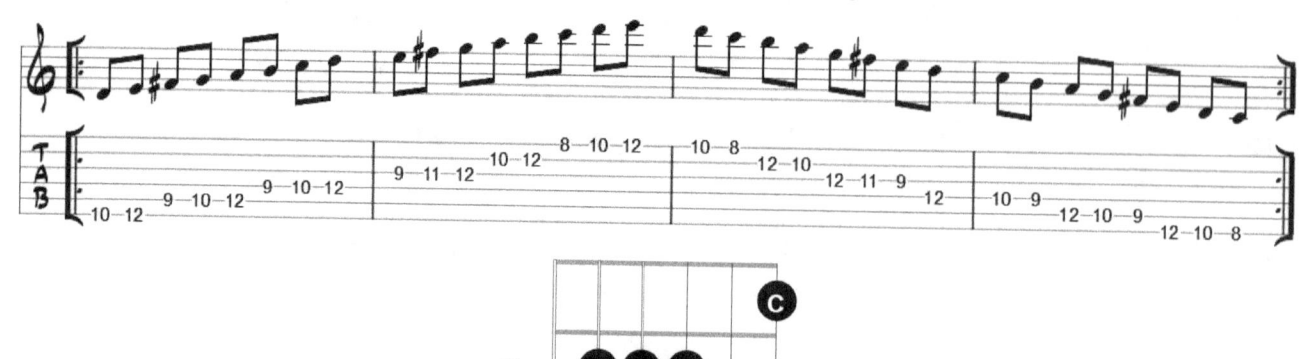

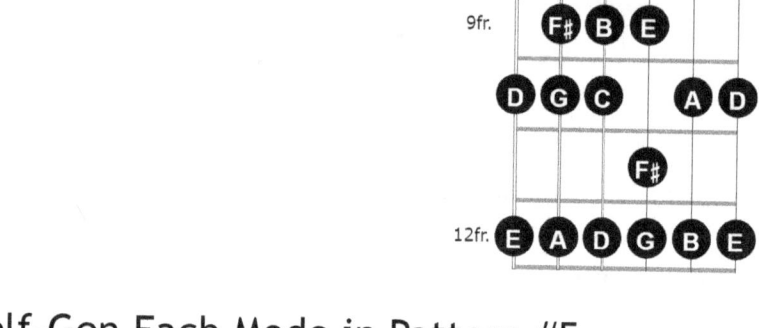

Self-Gen Each Mode in Pattern #5

Ascend and descend

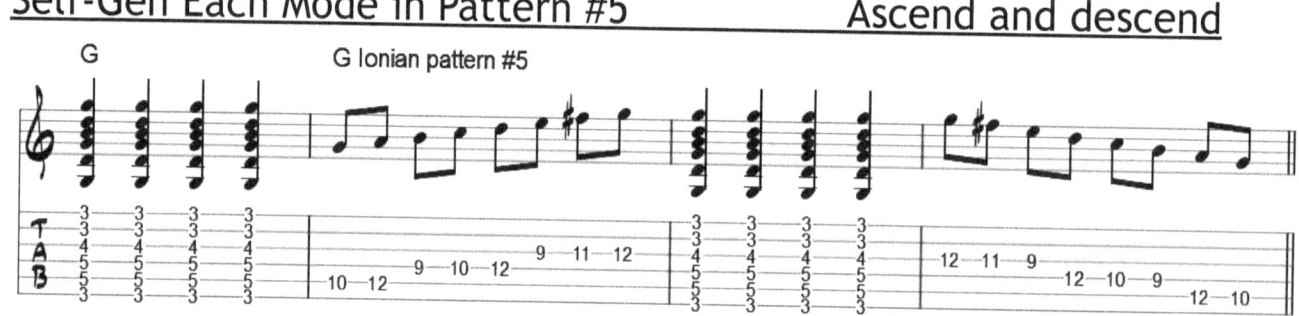

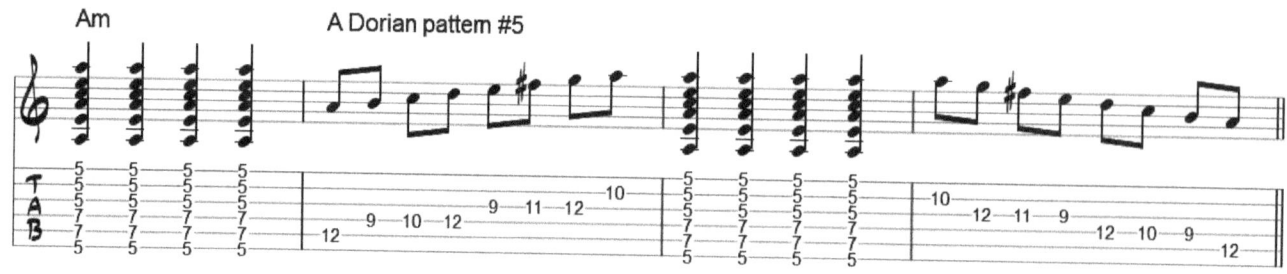

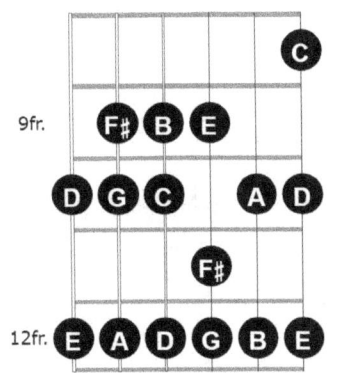

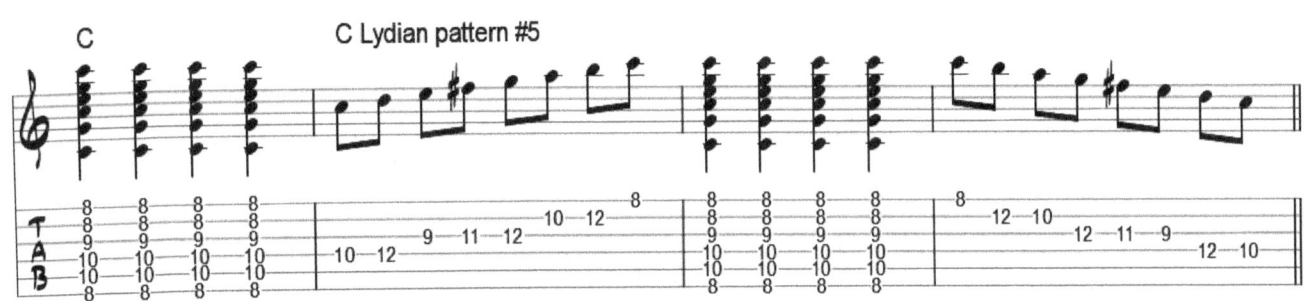

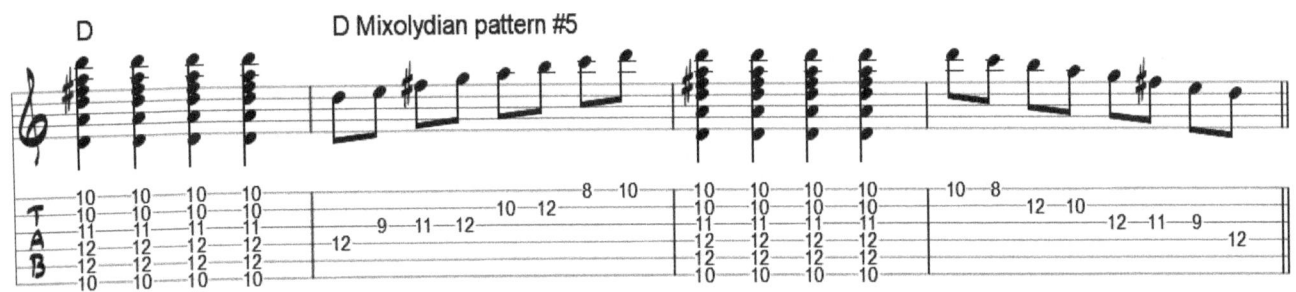

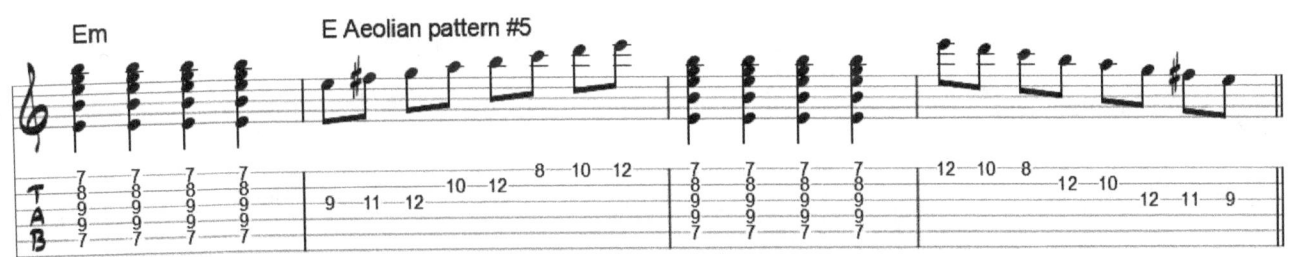

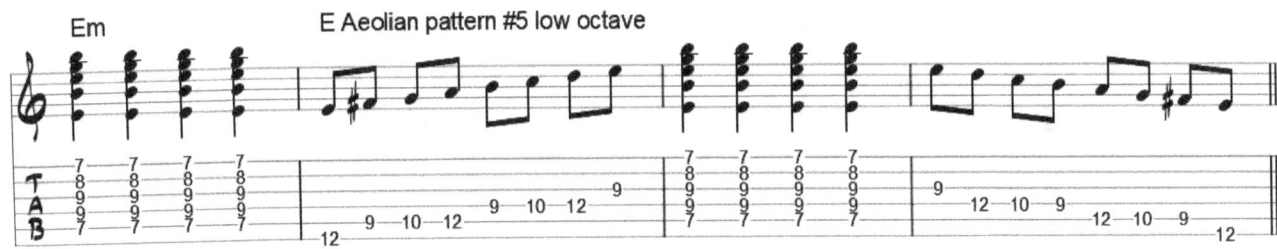

LICKS
"THE LICK" in all 5 patterns for E Aeolian

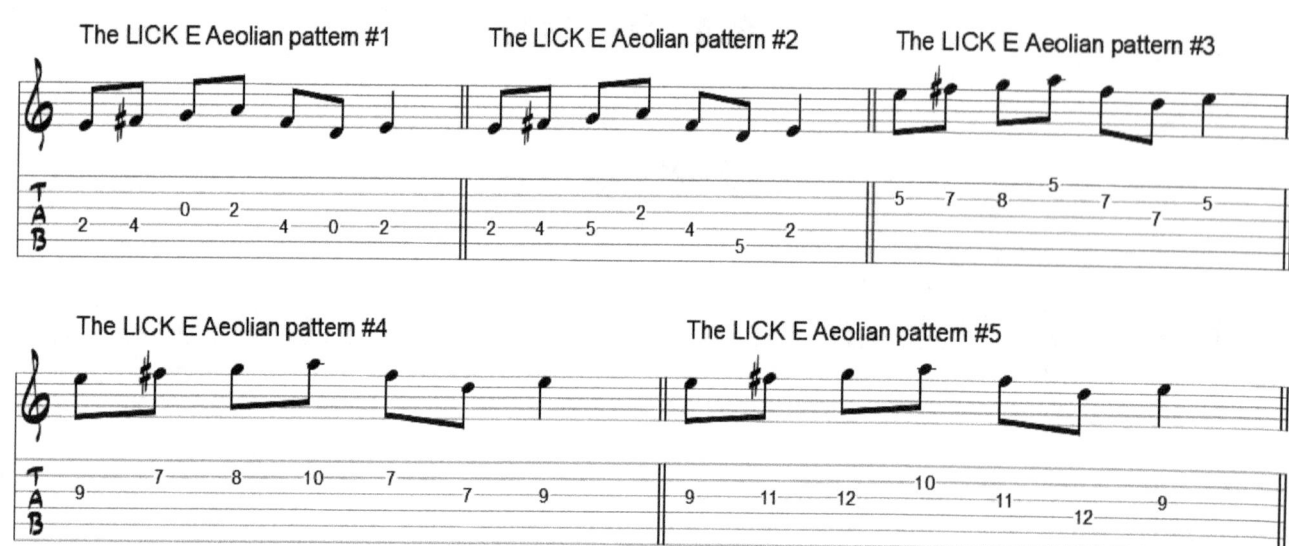

E Aeolian Bonus Lick in all 5 patterns

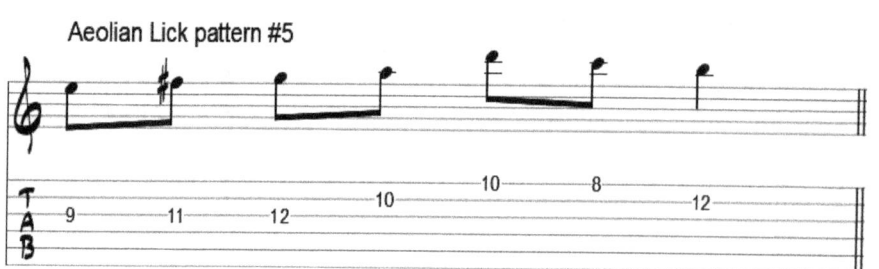

BACKING TRACKS

BACKING TRACKS
www.LeadGuitarWorkshop.com

G Ionian
|G |D |Em |C |

A Dorian
|Am |D |

B Phrygian
|Bm |C |

C Lydian
|C |D |

D Mixolydian
|D |C |G |D |

E Aeolian
|Em |D |Am |C |

SUMMARY

We are musicians. We are guitar players.
We learn the language of music. Melody, Harmony, and Rhythm
We learn the craft of playing the guitar as an instrument.

MODES are a function of a SCALE. You can start any scale on any one of its own notes. This is melody.

The MODES are: **Ionian, Dorian, Phrygian, Lydian, Mixolydian, Aeolian, Locrian.**

MODES are CHORD PROGRESSIONS. You can use any of the chords in a key to be the "main" chord, the TONIC. This is Harmony.

We learn to see common modal chord progressions

Diatonic Harmony = $\text{I ii iii IV V vi vii}^{\circ}$

As guitar players it is extremely helpful to see your octaves.

You will use ALL FIVE patterns for ALL 12 Keys, one for each fret. The patterns are always connected and in the same order, always. Whatever goes past the 12th fret reappears starting as open strings again. Like a giant conveyor belt.

Don't forget that at the 12th fret the guitar (an music world) starts over again an octave higher.

We use BACKING TRACKS and SELF GENERATE to give a real time context to our playing.

ALL 5 PATTERNS SOUND THE SAME. THEY ARE THE SAME SEVEN NOTES IN ANY GIVEN KEY. They help you use your whole fretboard.

CHAPTER 7

TUNE IN

"I am a musician and a guitar player. Music is my language and my guitar is my voice. Music is Melody, Harmony and Rhythm. I develop my language skills and my instrument skills. They are two separate worlds working together to complete the circle of music."

Rhythm is the number one factor to sounding great as a musician.

REVIEW

As a Musician:

- Modes happen as melodies
- Any one of the seven notes in the scale can be the ROOT.
- Modes happen as chord progressions
- Any one of the seven chords can be the "main" chord
- The notes in the key of G are: G A B C D E F#
- The chords in the Key of G are: G Am Bm C D Em (F#dim)
- The modes in the key of G are: G Ionian, A Dorian, B Phrygian, C Lydian, D Mixolydian, E Aeolian

As a Guitar Player:

- Added two notes to the five pentatonic shapes in the Key of G.
- Mapped shapes out across from open strings to 12th fret.
- Each pattern is two octaves of the notes in the key of G (and all its modes).
- Each pattern sounds the same as it is the same notes as the others.

WARM UP

Play each pattern ascending and descending. Pick a tempo and rhythm.

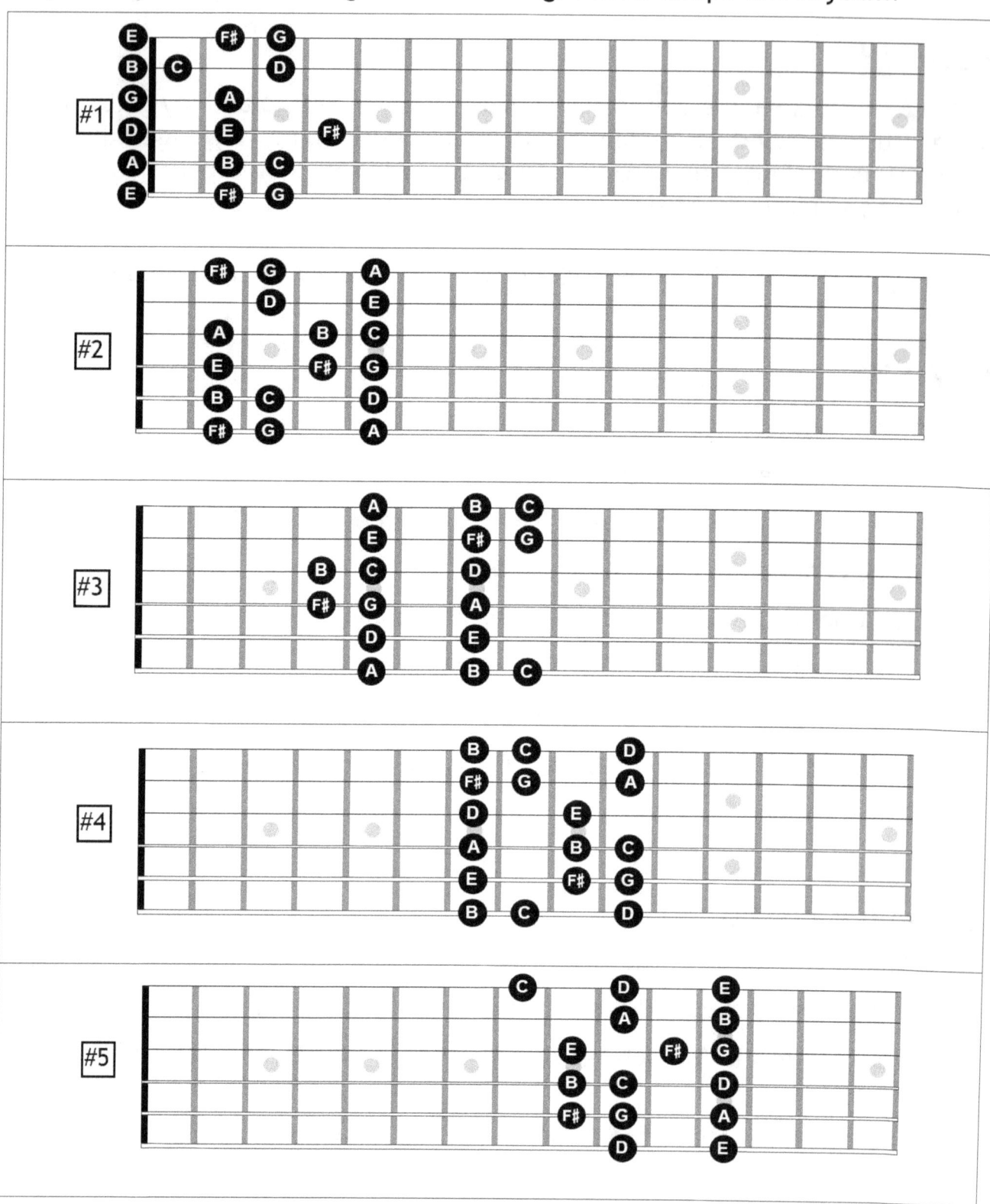

EXERCISE

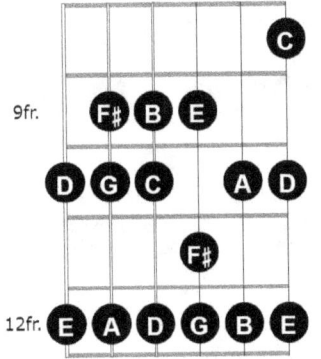

Self-Gen Each Mode in Pattern #5   Ascend and descend

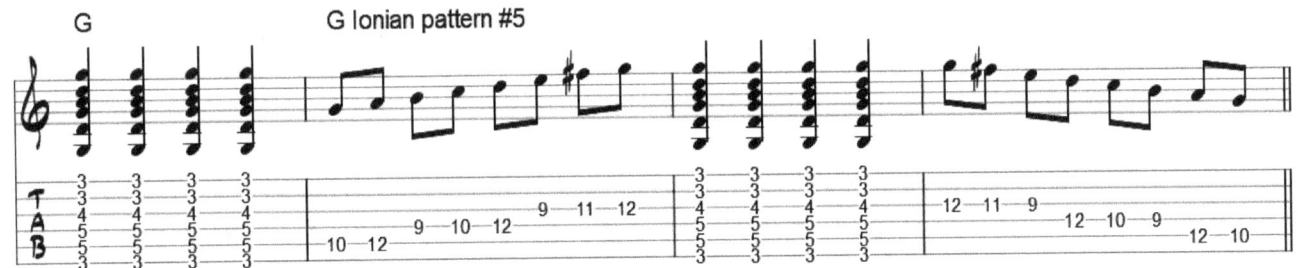

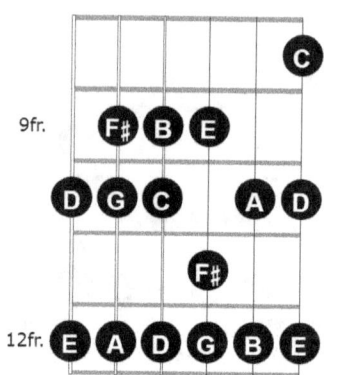

C — C Lydian pattern #5

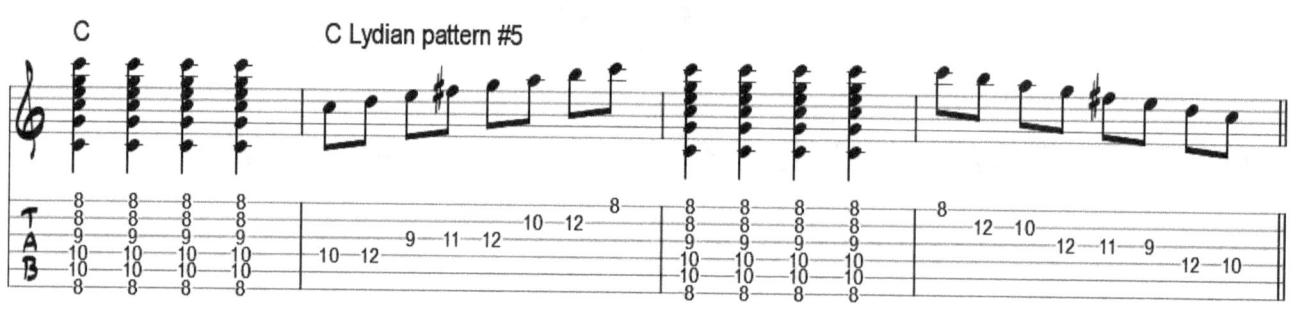

D — D Mixolydian pattern #5

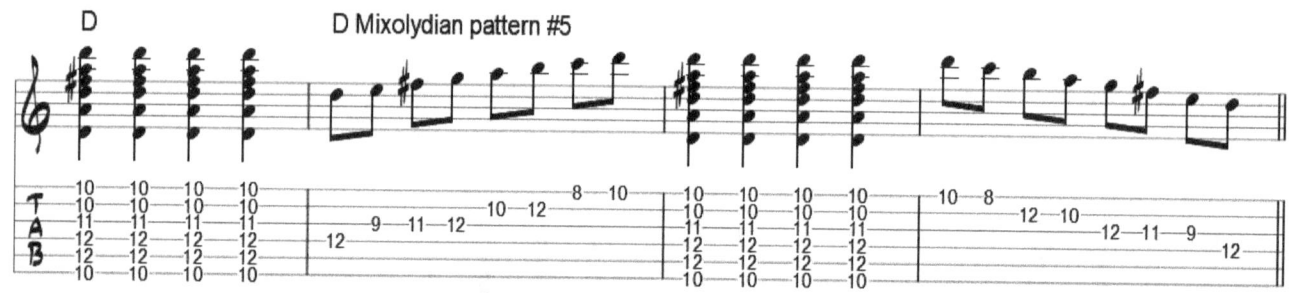

Em — E Aeolian pattern #5

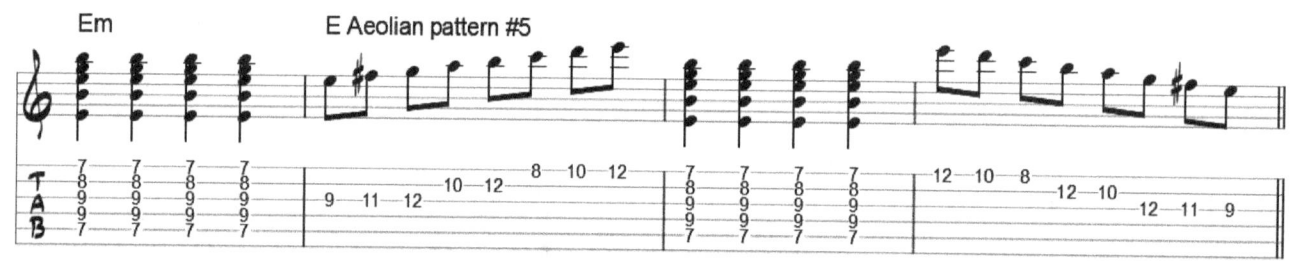

Em — E Aeolian pattern #5 low octave

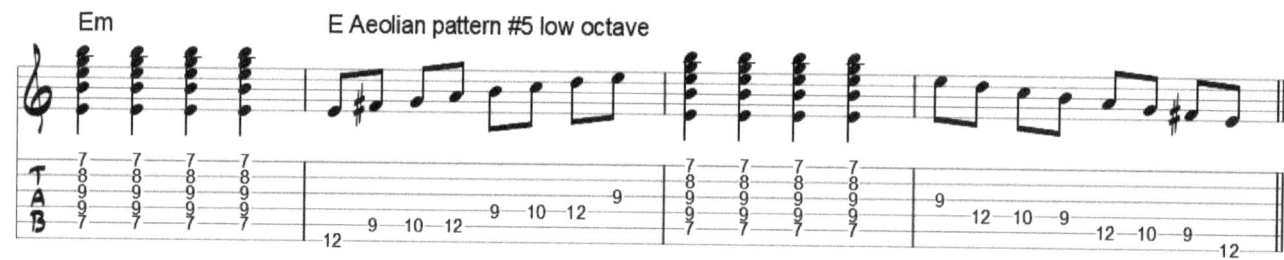

SCALE SPELLING

Another way to understand and think about the sound of modes as scales is to compare them when they have the SAME ROOT. This means they are coming from different keys.

For example if you compared a C IONIAN: C D E F G A B (key of C Major)

and a C DORIAN: C D Eb F G A Bb *(Key of Bb Major)*

you can see that the THIRD and SEVENTH are flattened in C Dorian. This establishes it as a minor scale. All MINOR MODES have a FLATTENED THIRD and SEVENTH.

The notes highlighted in GRAY are the characteristic note of that mode that help it sound unique from the other modes especially of the same type (Major vs minor). Notice how the the characteristic note is often the half steps we added to make it a seven note scale.

Mode	SCALE SPELLING						
Ionian	R	2	3	4	5	6	7
Dorian	R	2	b3	4	5	6	b7
Phrygian	R	b2	b3	4	5	b6	b7
Lydian	R	2	3	#4	5	6	7
Mixolydian	R	2	3	4	5	6	b7
Aeolian	R	2	b3	4	5	b6	b7
Locrian	R	b2	b3	4	b5	b6	b7
	All minor modes have *b*3 and *b*7- light gray is characteristic note						

A great way to hear the sound of this and to practice on the guitar is to use a single string and an open string. We are going to do this all with the ROOT note of E. You will use the LOW open E string to sustain the sound of the ROOT (reference) as you play the mode up and down the HIGH E string. You can map out WWHWWWH to get the IONIAN scale and then adjust according to the scale spelling. I call this ONE STRING MUSIC THEORY. It's easy to see and hear when it's all on one string. It is also super fun to go up and down on one string. It's very intuitive and also a great way to move on the guitar and get out of "positions."

ONE STRING MUSIC THEORY - MODES ALL WITH "E" ROOT

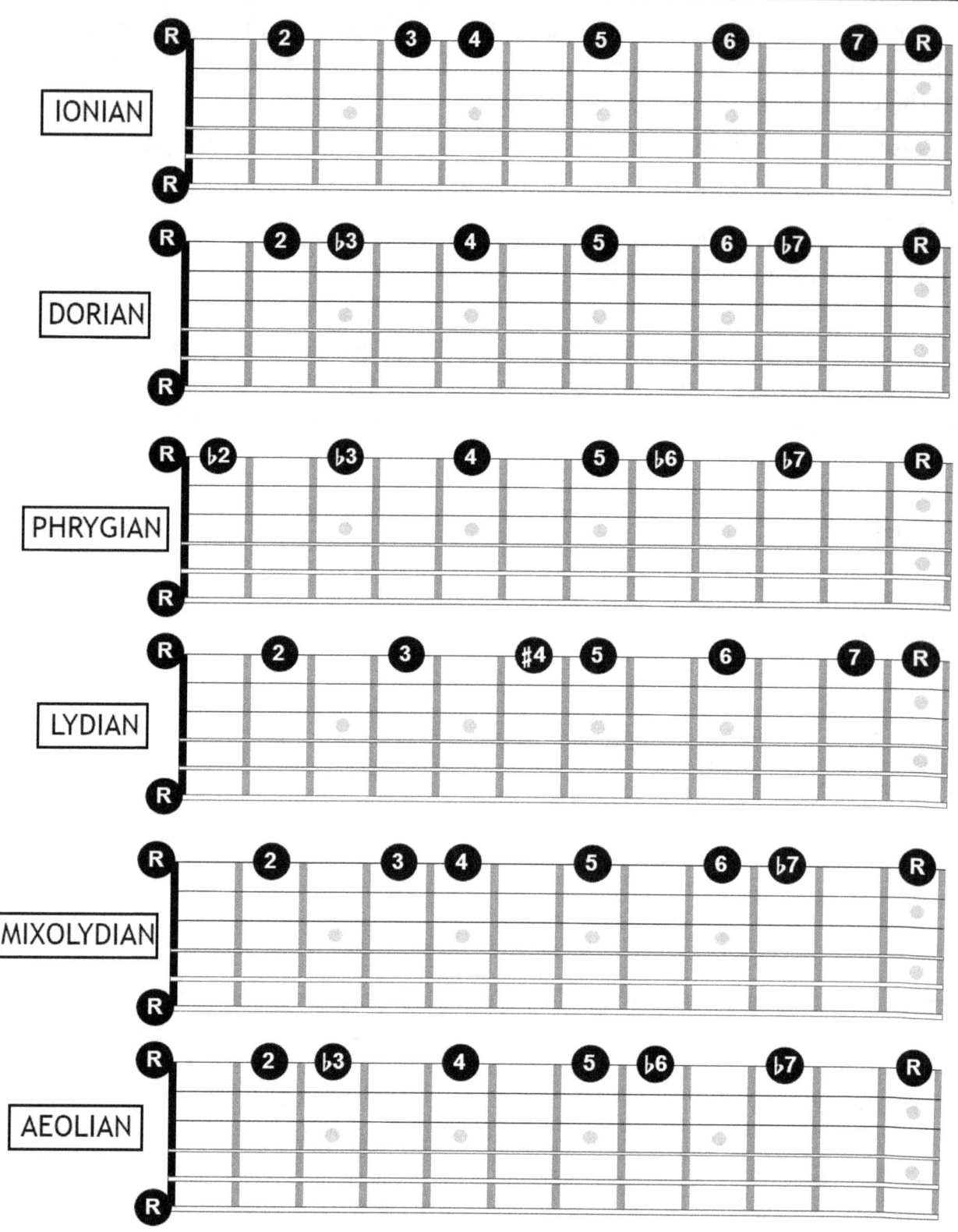

SEVENTH CHORDS

We have 12 notes, that you can apply the WWHWWWH formula to make the Ionian scale. From there we apply the RULE OF THIRDS and stack every other note for a total of three notes to make a triad. We do this from each of the seven notes in the scale to create the seven DIATONIC TRIADS.

G	G A B C D E F# G A B C D E F#
Am	G A B C D E F# G A B C D E F#
Bm	G A B C D E F# G A B C D E F#
C	G A B C D E F# G A B C D E F#
D	G A B C D E F# G A B C D E F#
Em	G A B C D E F# G A B C D E F#
F#dim	G A B C D E F# G A B C D E F#

Each Chord will have its own ROOT, THIRD and FIFTH.

5	D	E	F#	G	A	B	C
3	B	C	D	E	F#	G	A
R	G	A	B	C	D	E	F#

When we use the RULE OF THIRDS to stack THREE notes they are called TRIADS. What do you call it when you do it for FOUR NOTES?
SEVENTH CHORDS of course! What? Why is that so confusing?
Triads are named after how many notes are in the chord. Seventh chords are named by the degree in the scale away from the Root that you stopped stacking.
If you stack every other note for four notes we will get all the SEVENTH CHORDS for the Key. They have the same Major and minor qualities but with more color and definition than just the TRIAD.

GMaj7	G A B C D E F# G A B C D E F#
Am7	G A B C D E F# G A B C D E F#
Bm7	G A B C D E F# G A B C D E F#
CMaj7	G A B C D E F# G A B C D E F#
D7	G A B C D E F# G A B C D E F#
Em7	G A B C D E F# G A B C D E F#
F#m7b5	G A B C D E F# G A B C D E F#

Now each chord will have a ROOT, THIRD, FIFTH, and SEVENTH note.

7	F#	G	A	B	C	D	E
5	D	E	F#	G	A	B	C
3	B	C	D	E	F#	G	A
R	G	A	B	C	D	E	F#

Seventh chords have a more defined sound. Triads are a little more cut and dry. There are FOUR TYPES of SEVENTH CHORDS: *MAJOR 7, DOMINANT 7, MINOR 7, and MINOR 7 FLAT FIVE (aka Half Diminished) (rarely used).*

MAJOR SEVENTH (Maj7) chords are what I call "Green grassy field" Chords. Just lay back and watch the clouds go by. They sound soft, innocent. There are two Maj7 chords per key the I and the IV (Ionian and Lydian)

DOMINANT SEVENTH (7) There is *ONLY ONE PER KEY* and it is the V (Mixolydian). These chords sound brash and bluesy.

MINOR SEVENTH (m7) chords sound "cool." They are hipper sounding than just a minor triad which sounds solemn. All three minor chords become m7.

Triads	I	ii	iii	IV	V	vi	vii dim
	I Major	ii minor	iii minor	IV Major	V Major	vi minor	vii dim
7th Chords	I Maj7	iim7	iiim7	IV Maj7	V7	vim7	vii-7b5
Modes	Ionian	Dorian	Phrygian	Lydian	Mixolydian	Aeolian	Locrian
DEGREE	TONIC	SUPER TONIC	MEDIANT	SUB DOMINANT	DOMINANT	SUB MEDIANT	LEADING TONE
SOUND	Relative MAJOR*	Happy minor	Dark+Heavy minor	Exotic Major	Funky Major	Relative MINOR*	dark and dim
KEYS 5ths ⬇	C	D	E	F	G	A	B
	G	A	B	C	D	E	F#
	D	E	F#	G	A	B	C#
	A	B	C#	D	E	F#	G#
	E	F#	G#	A	B	C#	D#
	B	C#	D#	E	F#	G#	A#
	Gb/F#	Ab/G#	Bb/A#	Cb/B	Db/C#	Eb/D#	F/E#
	Db	Eb	F	Gb	Ab	Bb	C
	Ab	Bb	C	Db	Eb	F	G
	Eb	F	G	Ab	Bb	C	D
	Bb	C	D	Eb	F	G	A
⬆ 4ths	F	G	A	Bb	C	D	E

PRACTICE

Self-Gen One String Music Theory - MODES

Use either E Major or E minor depending on the Mode. Play one bar of the chord and one bar of the scale. You should play the scale ascending and descending. You can go back to page 84 to follow visually.

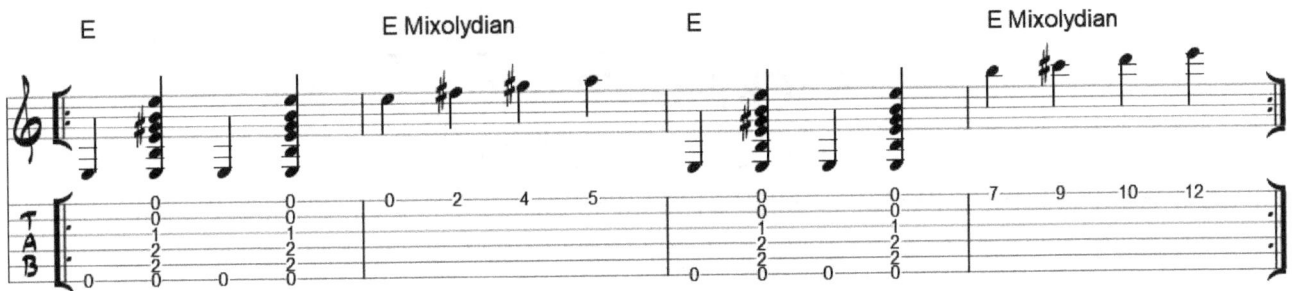

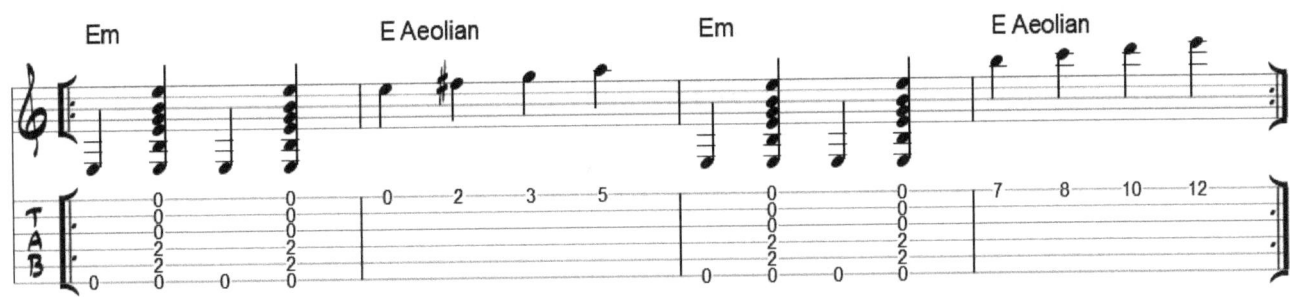

Make sure to keep the LOW E string ringing as a sonic reference. If you are quick, you can hit the low string right before you play the scale.

It's also really fun to play a little looser and just hit the low string and freely play up and down the string in a more musical way.

Playing on one string is really easy to look at. You can play sequences in a much more visual manner.

Keep in mind, that ANY E note you start on will work. You can practice looking at the intervals from the E note even though it's not on the open E string. In fact, if you were able to keep track of the notes on a single string up and down, and could then do it for each string, you would not need the patterns!

BACKING TRACKS

BACKING TRACKS
www.LeadGuitarWorkshop.com
G Ionian
|G |D |Em |C |
A Dorian
|Am |D |
B Phrygian
|Bm |C |
C Lydian
|C |D |
D Mixolydian
|D |C |G |D |
E Aeolian
|Em |D |Am |C |

SUMMARY

We are musicians. We are guitar players.
We learn the language of music. Melody, Harmony, and Rhythm
We learn the craft of playing the guitar as an instrument.

MODES are a function of a SCALE. You can start any scale on any one of its own notes. This is melody.

The MODES are: **Ionian, Dorian, Phrygian, Lydian, Mixolydian, Aeolian, Locrian.**

MODES are CHORD PROGRESSIONS. You can use any of the chords in a key to be the "main" chord, the TONIC. This is Harmony.

We learn to see common modal chord progressions. We look for TRIADS and SEVENTH chords to help us determine Key, Mode, and when there are NON DIATONIC Chords.

Diatonic Harmony = I_{Maj7} ii_{m7} iii_{m7} IV_{Maj7} V_7 vi_{m7} vii_{m7b5}

As guitar players it is extremely helpful to see your octaves.

You will use ALL FIVE patterns for ALL 12 Keys, one for each fret. The patterns are always connected and in the same order, always. Whatever goes past the 12th fret reappears starting as open strings again, like a giant conveyor belt.

We can use the ONE STRING MUSIC THEORY to help us see and hear the different intervals of the modes on one string. This also makes it easier to play on one string and not get stuck in just patterns.

Don't forget that at the 12th fret the guitar (an music world) starts over again an octave higher.

We use BACKING TRACKS and SELF GENERATE to give a real time context to our playing.

ALL 5 PATTERNS SOUNDS THE SAME IN ANY GIVEN KEY. THEY ARE THE SAME SEVEN NOTES. They help you use your whole fretboard.

CHAPTER 8

TUNE IN

"I am a musician and a guitar player. Music is my language and my guitar is my voice. Music is Melody, Harmony and Rhythm. I develop my language skills and my instrument skills. They are two separate worlds working together to complete the circle of music."

Rhythm is the number one factor to sounding great as a musician.

It's so helpful to relate new music learning to music you already listen to and play. Every song you have ever listened to is in a key and a mode. This is based on the chords and scale. Once you start looking at your favorite music, you will start to see patterns. For example, certain artists stay in certain keys and like specific modes (The Grateful Dead, The Rolling Stones and ACDC all love Mixolydian.) Certain songs have a specific mood. That might be because of the mode. You will learn so much once you start relating music you know and play, to the keys and modes they come from.

It's a habit and it takes practice and consistency. For every song you start to learn focus on the first chord, then think of the three keys it comes from. From there, chord by chord, look for the key and the modes.

The more songs you look at, analyze, and examine the more you will be able to memorize songs and be able to quickly identify the key and mode. There are only 12 keys. You will also cherish those songs that break the momentum of commonality and change keys and borrow chords. I use this all the time when writing and composing.

WARM UP

Play each pattern ascending and descending. Pick a tempo and rhythm.

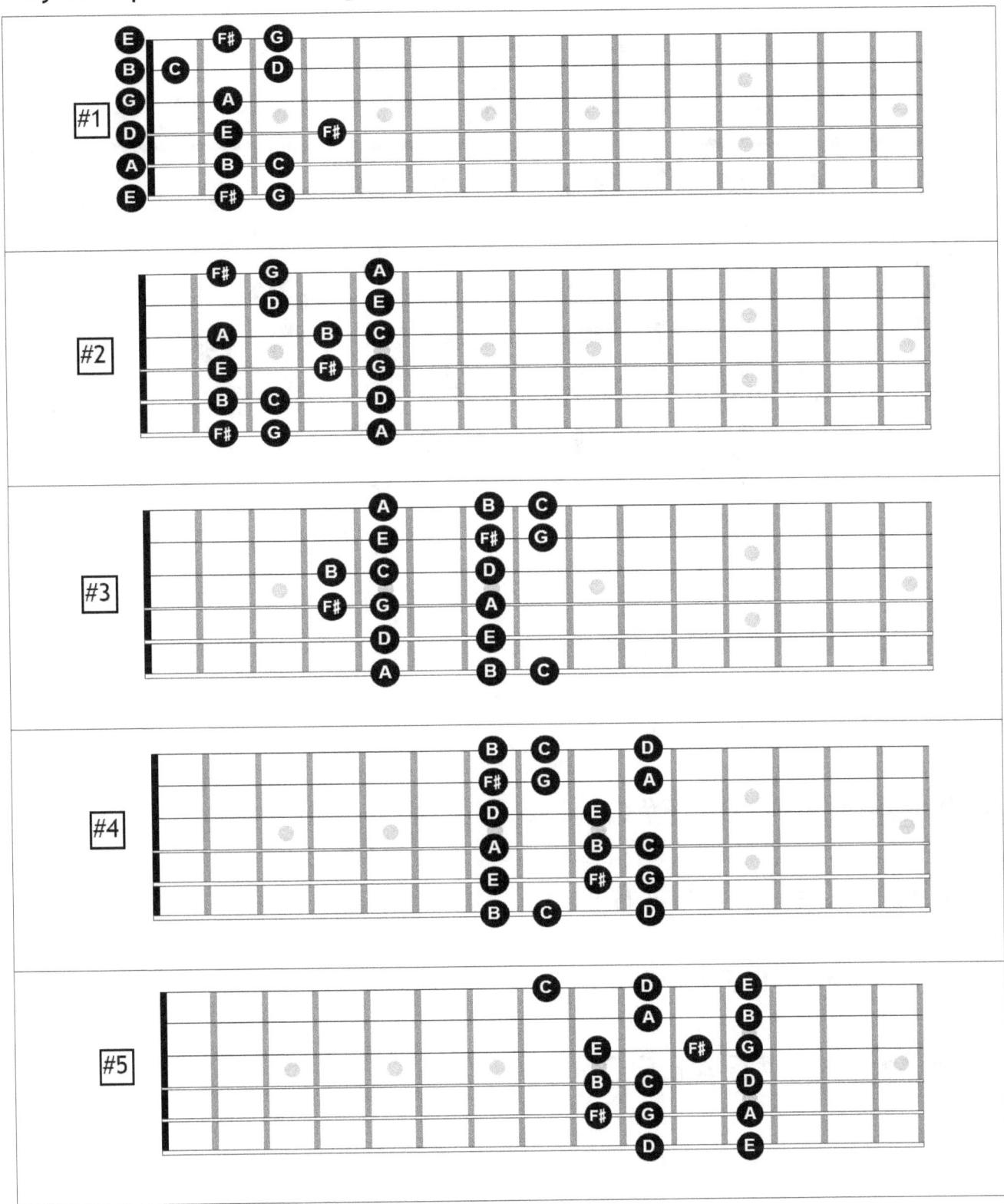

EXERCISE

Pick a pattern and play all the modes
or
pick a mode and play it in all the patterns

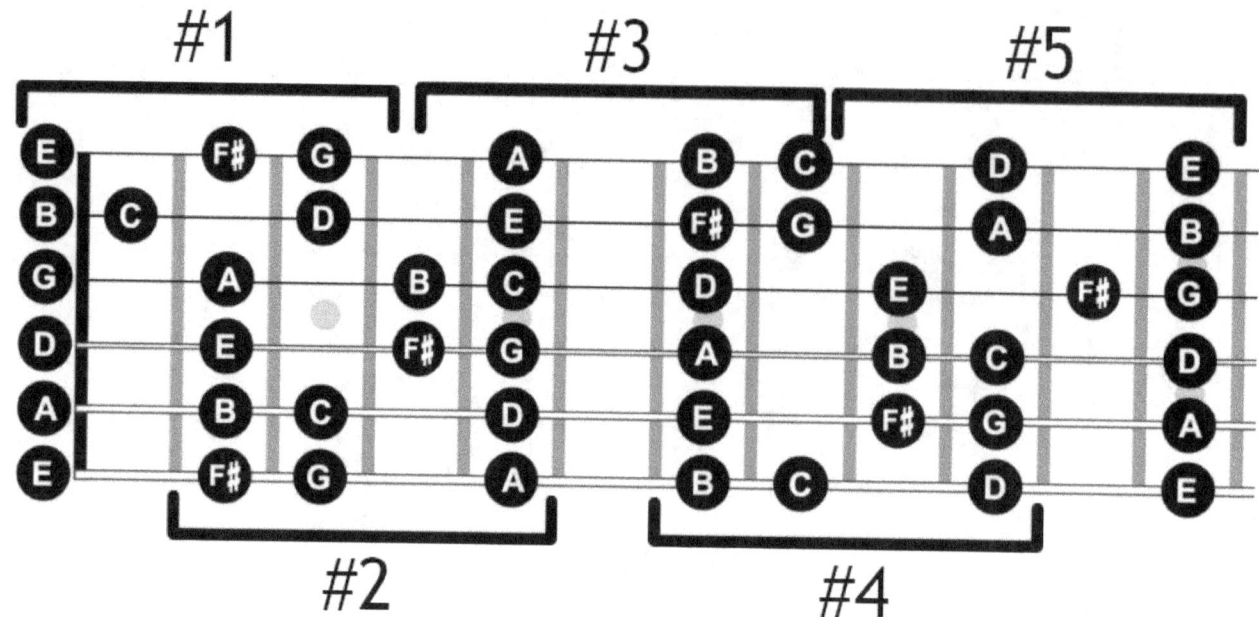

G Ionian: G A B C D E F#

A Dorian: A B C D E F# G

B Phrygian: B C D E F# G A

C Lydian: C D E F# G A B

D Mixolydian: D E F# G A B C

E Aeolian: E F# G A B C D

REVIEW

In the last chapter we looked at another way of thinking about the modes, musically speaking. Instead of thinking ONE Key and all of its modes (same seven notes, one key), we looked at keeping the ROOT *the same* and doing the modes from the *same note* (seven different keys!). When you compare modes from the same root note you can clearly hear a difference. Compare any mode to Ionian (of the same root) to see what notes are altered in that mode. For instance in all three minor modes (Dorian, Phrygian, and Aeolian) the THIRD and SEVENTH notes are always lowered (flattened) compared to Ionian.

Each mode has its own characteristics. Even though Ionian doesn't have a specific "Characteristic note", it is the addition of the HALF-STEPS to the pentatonic that give it it's sound. Upon deeper inspection, you would find that it is the two half-steps that are making all of the color in the modes. In the Key of G those two notes are C and F#.

Mode	SCALE SPELLING						
Ionian	R	2	3	4	5	6	7
Dorian	R	2	b3	4	5	6	b7
Phrygian	R	b2	b3	4	5	b6	b7
Lydian	R	2	3	#4	5	6	7
Mixolydian	R	2	3	4	5	6	b7
Aeolian	R	2	b3	4	5	b6	b7
Locrian	R	b2	b3	4	b5	b6	b7

All minor modes have *b3* and *b7*- light gray is characteristic note

Using your Low E string as a drone, you can build a mode from the open High E. The Ionian scale is WWHWWWH. From there, each one of the notes is numbers 1-7. Now go through and adjust for each mode (for example lower the third for minor etc)

LOCRIAN

What does it sound like to balance a triangle on it's tip? Locrian. Locrian is the last mode of the seven and it is definitely the least often used. It is based on a diminished triad and has a minor seven flat five chord (m7b5), also known as a "half-diminished" chord. It is very dark and unstable, both as a chord and a scale. In the Key of G it is an F# Locrian scale:

F# G A B C D E

The main issue with this chord and mode is that it has a flat five (b5) interval from the ROOT (F# to C). This means that you can't resolve to it, it needs to keep moving. If you look at just the F# diminished triad its F# A C. Those same notes are the upper three notes of a D7 chord, the Dominant. And like the D7, the F#dim chord wants to go home to the G Major chord. Diminished triads are written in one of two ways, as are the minor seven flat five chords (or the half-diminished).

Diminished TRIAD	
|F#dim	|F#o
Minor seven flat five/half-diminished SEVENTH CHORD	
|F#m7b5	|F#ø7

There are little to no songs that are based on Locrian, especially as a mode. There is "Inner Urge" by Joe Henderson and "Matrices" by Schleigho, but other than that, I have barley encountered it in the last 30 years. It's a cool and dark mood that's fun to explore. But, I would recommend focusing on the first six modes that are in use all of the time.

MODE LICKS BY THE NOTE

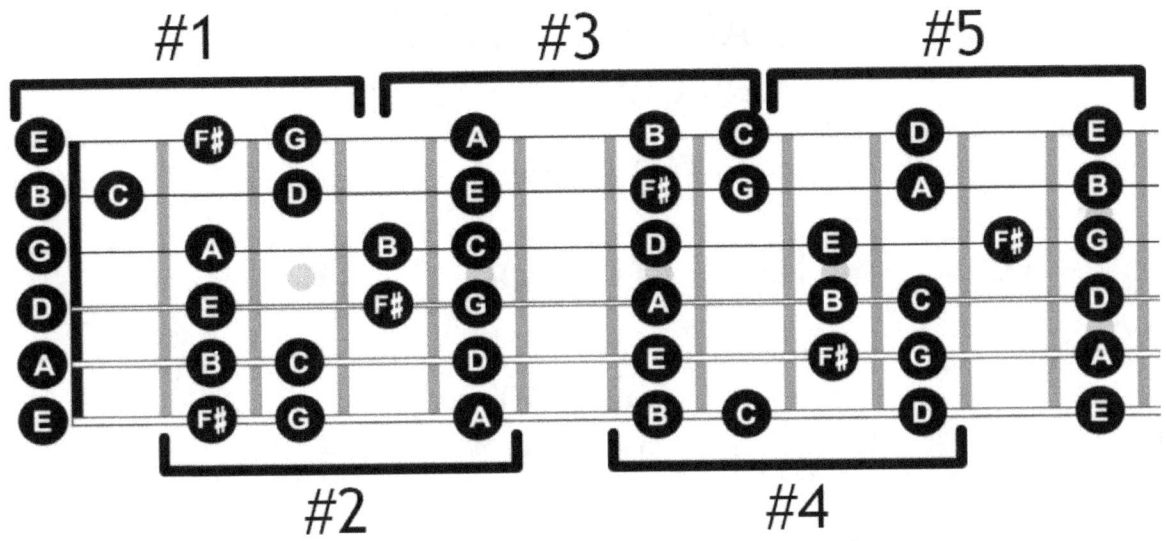

G Ionian:	#1 G A B C A F# G
	#2 G A B D F# E D
A Dorian:	#1 A B C D B G A
	#2 A C E G F# E
B Phrygian:	#1 B C D E D A B
	#2 B C D F# E F#
C Lydian:	#1 C D E F# D B C
	#2 C D E F# G F# G
D Mixolydian:	#1 D E F# G E C D
	#2 D B C A F#
E Aeolian:	#1 E F# G A F# D E
	#2 E G B D C B
F# Locrian:	#1 F# G A C B E F#

BACKING TRACKS

BACKING TRACKS
www.LeadGuitarWorkshop.com

G Ionian
|G |D |Em |C |

A Dorian
|Am |D |

B Phrygian
|Bm |C |

C Lydian
|C |D |

D Mixolydian
|D |C |G |D |

E Aeolian
|Em |D |Am |C |

F# Locrian
|F#m^{7b5} |

SUMMARY

As a Musician:

- Modes happen as melodies.

- Any one of the seven notes in the scale can be the ROOT.

- Modes happen as chord progressions.

- Any one of the seven chords can be the "main" chord.

- The notes in the key of G are: G A B C D E F#

- The chords in the Key of G are: G Am Bm C D Em (F#dim)

- The modes in the key of G are: **G Ionian, A Dorian, B Phrygian, C Lydian, D Mixolydian, E Aeolian, F# Locrian**

As a Guitar Player:

- Added two notes to the five pentatonic shapes in the Key of G.

- Mapped them out across from open strings to 12th fret.

- Each pattern is two octaves of the notes in the key of G (and all its modes).

- Each pattern sounds the same as it is the same notes as the others.

- The five patterns are ALWAYS in the same order.

- Use Pattern #1 "Rock and Roll Rule" to get IN THE KEY of any mode you are looking for.

We are musicians. We are guitar players.
We learn the language of music. Melody, Harmony, and Rhythm
We learn the craft of playing the guitar as an instrument.

CHAPTER 9

TUNE IN

"I am a musician and a guitar player. Music is my language and my guitar is my voice. Music is Melody, Harmony and Rhythm. I develop my language skills and my instrument skills. They are two separate worlds working together to complete the circle of music."

Rhythm is the number one factor to sounding great as a musician.

WARM UP

Play each pattern ascending and descending. Pick a tempo and rhythm.

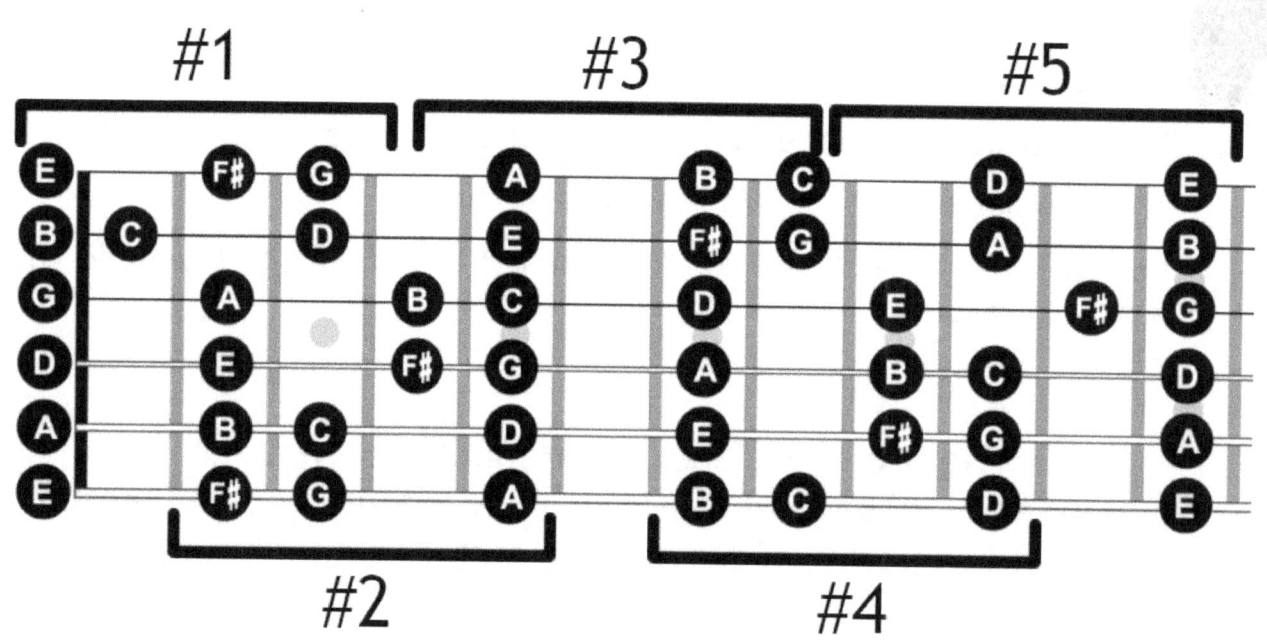

EXERCISE

Pick a pattern and play all the modes
or
pick a mode and play it in all the patterns

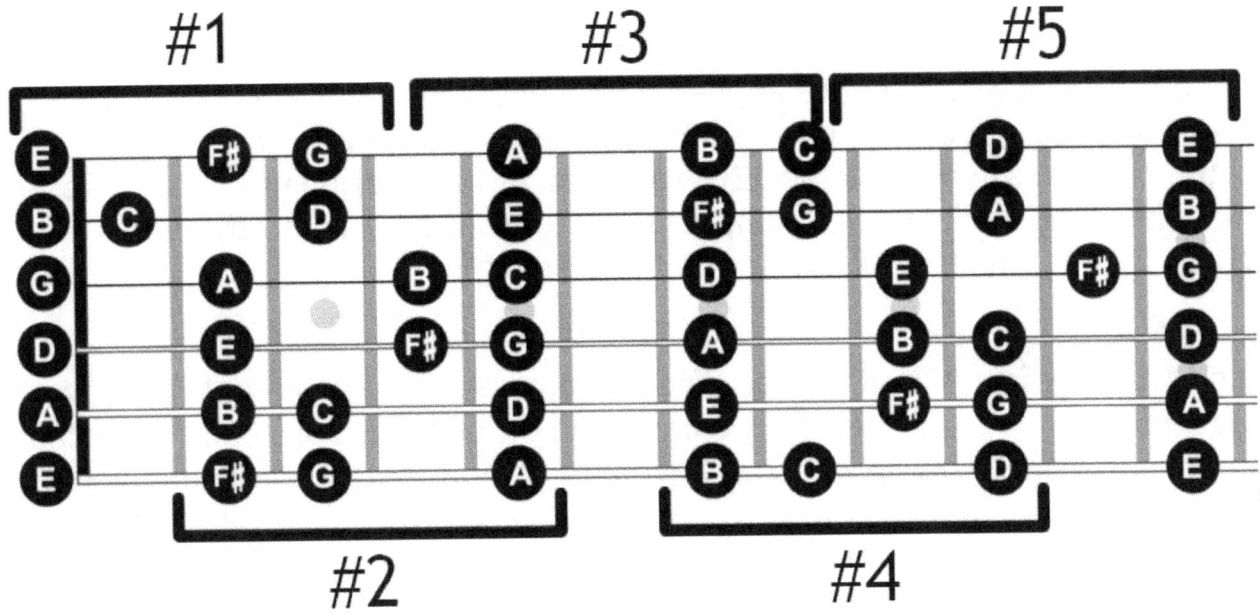

G Ionian: G A B C D E F#

A Dorian: A B C D E F# G

B Phrygian: B C D E F# G A

C Lydian: C D E F# G A B

D Mixolydian: D E F# G A B C

E Aeolian: E F# G A B C D

NECK ANATOMY SCALES

There are only two octave shapes, short and long and the keystone is ALWAYS

Short Octave to Long Octave

There are 12 notes. Any note appears only once on a string per 12 frets . You have 6 strings, so you will have 6 of any note on the first 12 frets of your guitar. As soon as you pass the 12th fret it all starts over again. It's a little tricky keeping track of the actual octaves. Unisons happen on the previous string, 5 frets higher (4 if you are on the B string).

Neck Anatomy is my term for this relationship. We have looked at it in level 2 and 3 and now we will see how we can build all of our MODE scales with the same knowledge. This approach is how most instruments play. Ideally you use the same fingers in the same way for each octave of notes. Only the guitar and other stringed instruments have this really difficult way of looking at notes in position, cutting against the grain of the momentum of the notes. This makes each pattern look and feel completely different than the others, even though they are the EXACT SAME NOTES.

Here are G Notes looking at the fretboard Short Octave to Long Octave. These are like fence posts. We can build the same scale in the same way from each one. It should feel, act and respond the same way in each and any octave.

Everything repeats
At 12th fret

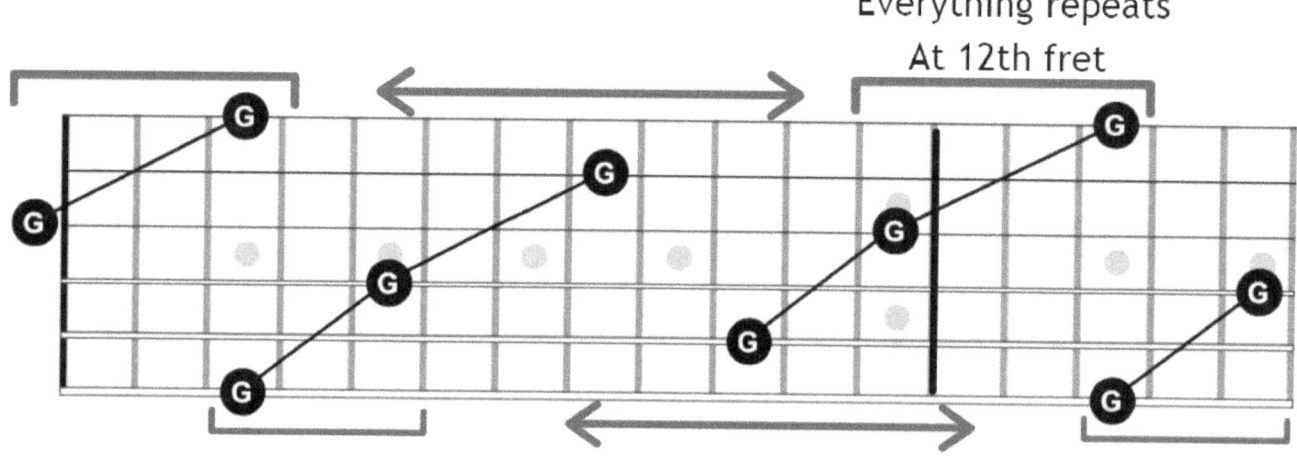

Neck Anatomy 7 Natural Notes

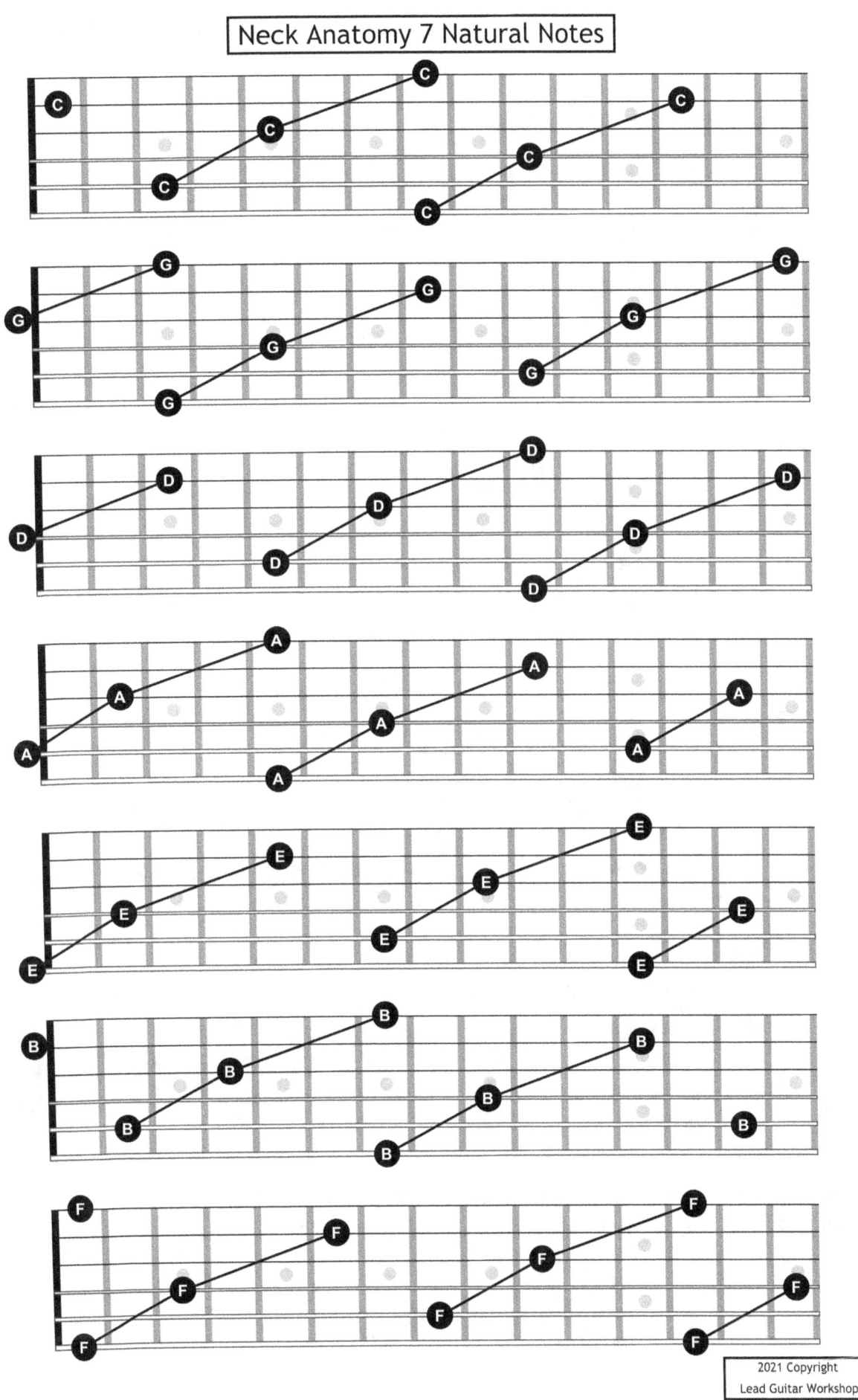

If we start with a G note and build a G Ionian scale we can see that it uses the familiar 1 2 4 Stretch shape of the SHELLS. You will do two of those same shell shapes to get the first 6 notes of the scale. Then, there is a first finger shift to a half step below the next octave.

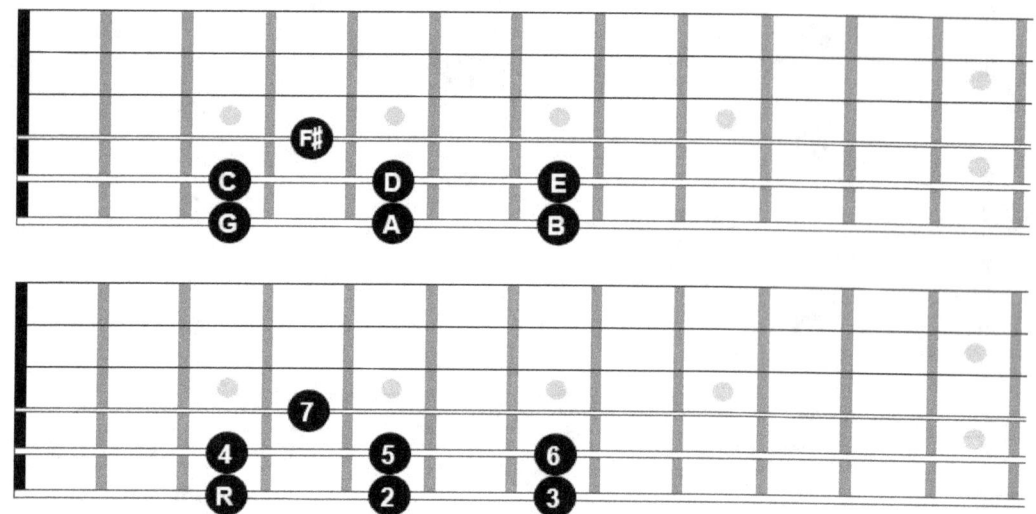

It is really helpful and important that you see the INTERVALS of the scale. Now all you have to do is pick up the scale and move it to the next octave, or any G ROOT note.

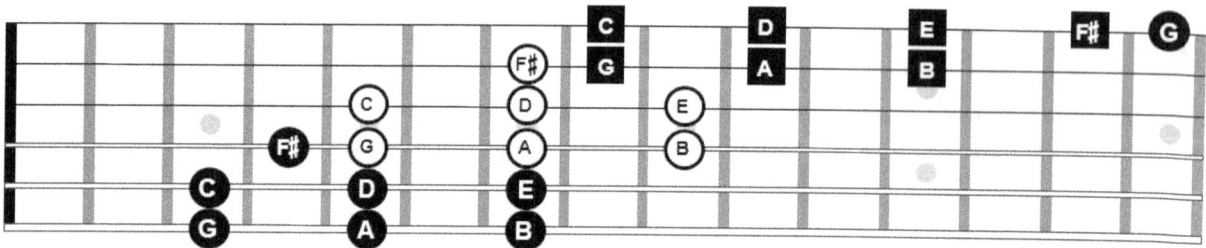

Keep in mind that the **B string requires you to move the notes up 1 fret** to compensate for it being tuned to the third instead of a fourth.

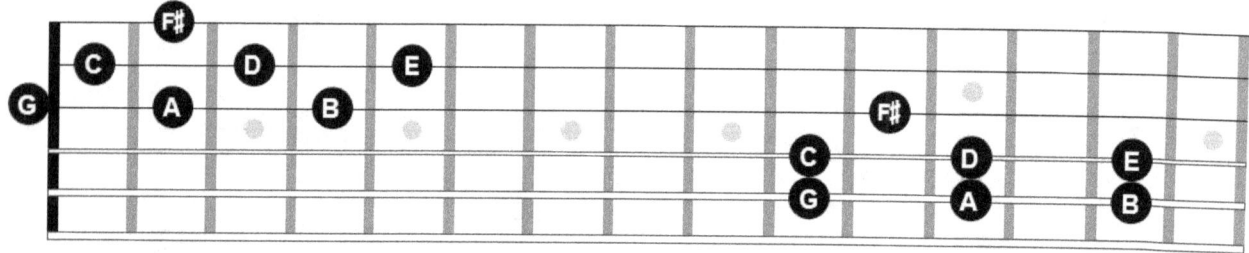

Always keep an eye on the octaves. Notice how the notes/intervals relate to the ROOT. You can play ONE Shape from ALL of the G notes!

NECK ANATOMY 7 MODE Patterns by Intervals

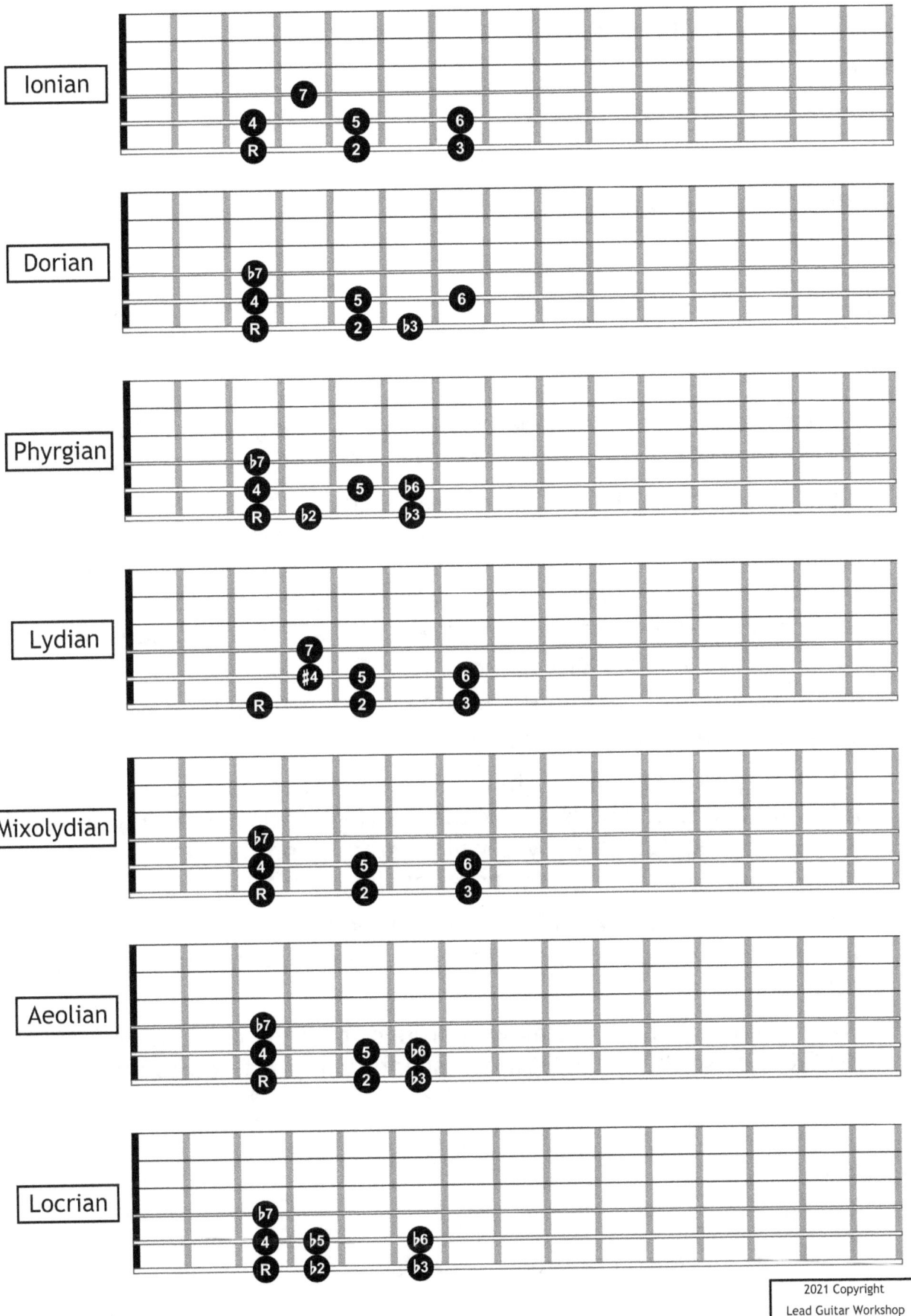

PRACTICE

In the Key of G go through each mode

G Ionian

A Dorian

B Phrygian

C Lydian

D Mixolydian

E Aeolian

F# Locrian

1. Locate the ROOT of the mode on the LOW E string and build the first SHORT to LONG OCTAVE to get the first 3 of all 6 mode root notes.

2. Play the appropriate MODE shape from each of these 3 Octaves. The middle shape will need to be compensated on the B string by 1 fret. The highest Octave can only play 6 of the 7 notes. For the final note just move up the E string after the 6th note to find the 7th note. The best way is to remember the relationship between the 7th of the mode and the ROOT (half or whole-step)

3. Go to the A string and find the ROOT NOTE and build the SHORT to LONG OCTAVE shapes to get the last 3 of 6 notes.

4. Play the appropriate MODE shape from each of those 3 octaves. As usual you will have to compensate for the B string by moving everything up 1 fret. In the Highest octave you will be starting on the High E string so you will only get the first few notes of the scale.

5. Play each scale as QUARTER-NOTES and focus on moving your whole hand at once to move to the next octave. You have to widen your peripheral vision.

6. Once you are comfortable moving around, pick the correlating BACKING TRACK and use the NECK ANATOMY shapes you practiced to solo with.

BACKING TRACKS

BACKING TRACKS
PLAY ALONG BACKING TRACK
www.LeadGuitarWorkshop.com

G Ionian

| |G | |D | |Em | |C | |

A Dorian

| |Am | |D | |

B Phrygian

| |Bm | |C | |

C Lydian

| |C | |D | |

D Mixolydian

| |D | |C | |G | |D | |

E Aeolian

| |Em | |D | |Am | |C | |

F# Locrian

| |F#m7b5 | |

SUMMARY

We are musicians. We are guitar players.
We learn the language of music. Melody, Harmony, and Rhythm
We learn the craft of playing the guitar as an instrument.

MODES are a function of A SCALE. You can start any scale on any one of its own notes. This is melody.

The MODES are: **Ionian, Dorian, Phrygian, Lydian, Mixolydian, Aeolian, Locrian.**

MODES are CHORD PROGRESSIONS. You can use any of the chords in a key to be the "main" chord, the TONIC. This is Harmony.

We learn to see common modal chord progressions. We look for TRIADS and SEVENTH chords to help us determine Key, Mode, and when there are NON DIATONIC Chords.

Diatonic Harmony = I_{Maj7} ii_{m7} iii_{m7} IV_{Maj7} V_7 vi_{m7} vii_{m7b5}

As guitar players it is extremely helpful to see your octaves.

You will use ALL FIVE patterns for ALL 12 Keys. The patterns are always connected and in the same order, always. Whatever goes past the 12th fret reappears starting as open strings again, like a giant conveyor belt.

We can use the ONE STRING MUSIC THEORY to help us see and hear the different intervals of the modes on one string. This also makes it easier to play on one string and not get stuck in just patterns.

NECK ANATOMY is the gateway to using your whole fretboard in a very musical and consistent way, like other instruments. You just need to memorize one (7) note pattern and move it to all the OCTAVES and play it in the same way.

We use BACKING TRACKS and SELF GENERATE to give a real time context to our playing.

ALL 5 PATTERNS SOUNDS THE SAME IN ANY GIVEN KEY.
THEY ARE THE SAME SEVEN NOTES.

CHAPTER 10

TUNE IN

"I am a musician and a guitar player. Music is my language and my guitar is my voice. Music is Melody, Harmony and Rhythm. I develop my language skills and my instrument skills. They are two separate worlds working together to complete the circle of music."

Rhythm is the number one factor to sounding great as a musician.

WARM UP

Pick a tempo and a rhythm.

Ascend and descend each pattern.

Play them as "Round the Block" (ascend pattern #1, shift up, descend pattern #2, shift up, ascend pattern #3 and continue in that manner).

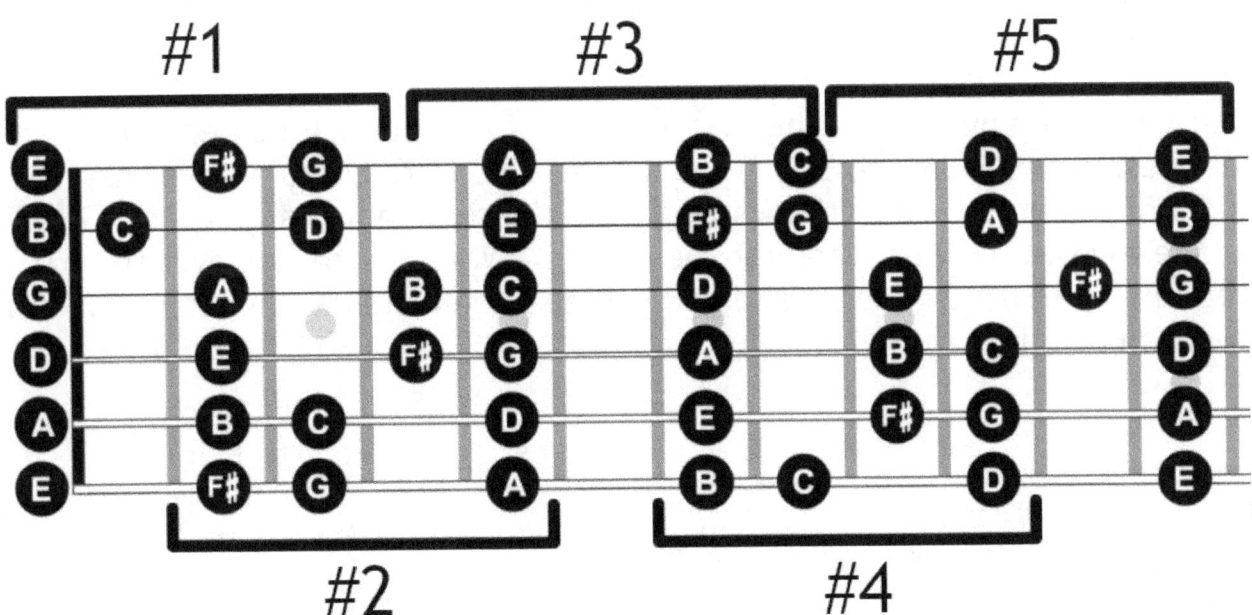

NECK ANATOMY SCALES

Looking at the guitar relative to its octaves is a great way to navigate our modes instead of using the traditional cross cut patterns. One way to see our notes is in a barber pole fashion. When you look at them at angles with SHORT OCTAVE to LONG OCTAVE you can use just one, seven note shape, to play all the octaves and positions on your fretboard.

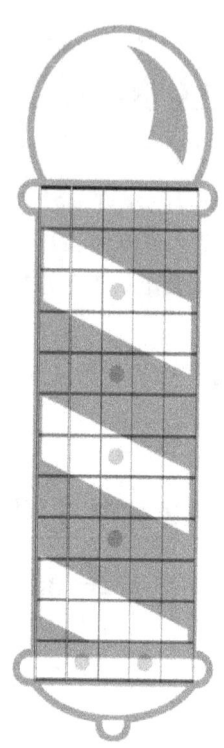

Most other instruments learn one way to play a seven note scale and then move by the octaves. A piano player just moves their hand up 12 keys and the same scale is played the same way with the same fingers (usually). It feels, looks, acts, and sounds the same in every octave. On saxophones there is an octave button on the back. For flute you just blow a little tighter and the notes go up an octave. They all basically play the same notes in the same way for each octave of the instrument's range.

Guitar players are like piano players in 3D. We move notes left and right like a piano does but we also move them forward and backward creating a redundancy of notes and a very visually confusing look.

There are 6 of any note on the first 12 frets of the guitar (one per string per 12 notes/frets). From the Low E you make a SHORT to LONG octave shape to find 3 of the notes. Go to the A string, find the same note, and make a SHORT octave to LONG octave shape for the other 3. Whatever passes over the 12th fret will be an octave higher and you will also see it repeat an octave lower in the open position.

Everything repeats
At 12th fret

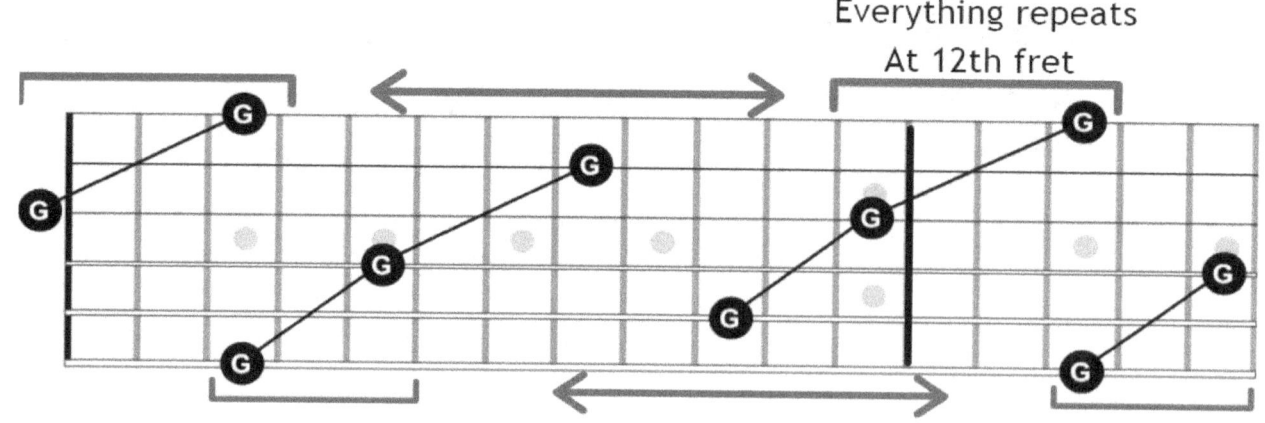

Once you find all of the octaves you can build scales from them, playing the same shape for every root note. There are only two things to consider.

1. You have to accommodate for the B string. It is tuned by 1 fret less than the other strings. Therefore you have to over compensate and move everything up 1 fret on the B string.
2. You will eventually run out of strings. Sometimes you just won't be able to complete the scale in the position you are in.

The following illustrations of the first six modes in the key of G
STARTING FROM 6TH STRING ROOT.

You continue Short to Long octave again on the A string to fill in the fretboard. In the big picture, your mode notes are over your entire fretboard, it's not select positions. These diagrams illustrate just part of this process. (They don't illustrate when you start from the A string).

1. You can see the notes of the Mode in white that are moving in the Neck Anatomy fashion. Each one follows the ROOT of the MODE by SHORT to LONG OCTAVE.
2. You will notice that I boxed the first 6 notes. To me it's really easy to see and remember this box and remember the 7th note as how it relates to the next ROOT. Only IONIAN and LYDIAN have a natural 7th note. That means it is a HALF-STEP below the next OCTAVE. MIXOLYDIAN, ALL THREE MINOR modes and LOCRIAN ALL have a FLAT 7, meaning it is a WHOLE-STEP below the ROOT.
3. Play the box of 6, then play the 7th note and shift up with the first finger into the new octave (start of the next box) to complete a seven note scale.

G IONIAN

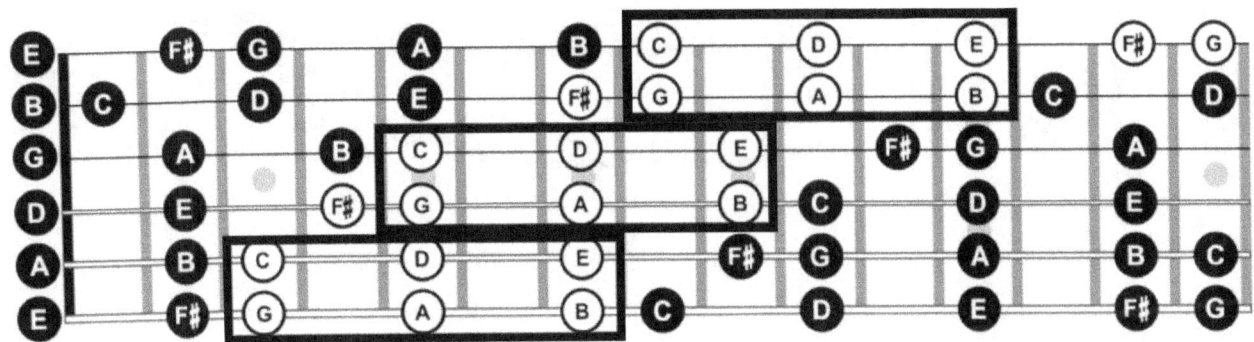

A DORIAN

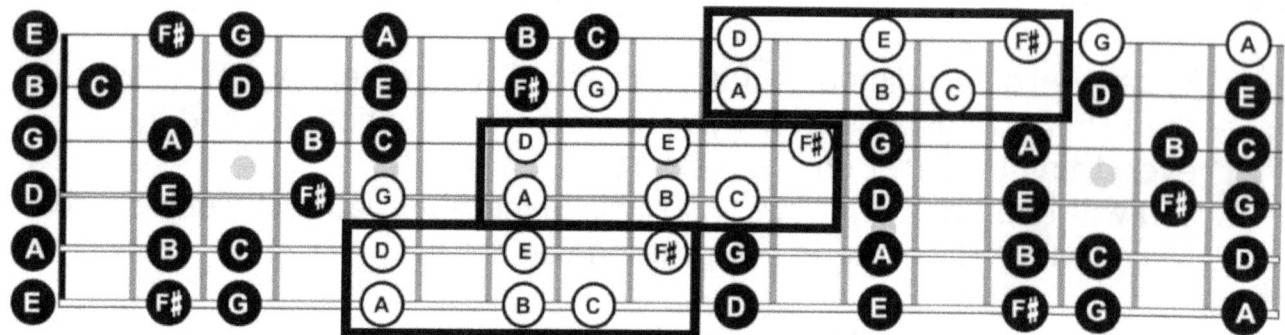

B PHRYGIAN

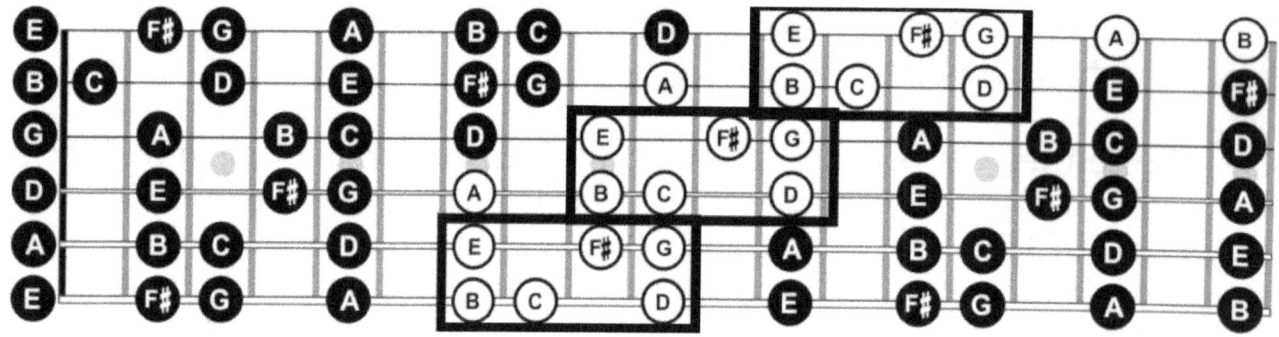

C LYDIAN

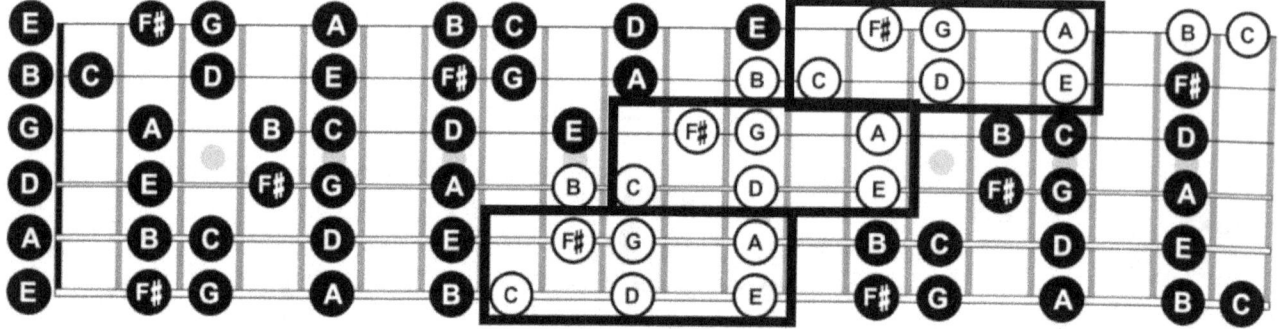

D MIXOLYDIAN

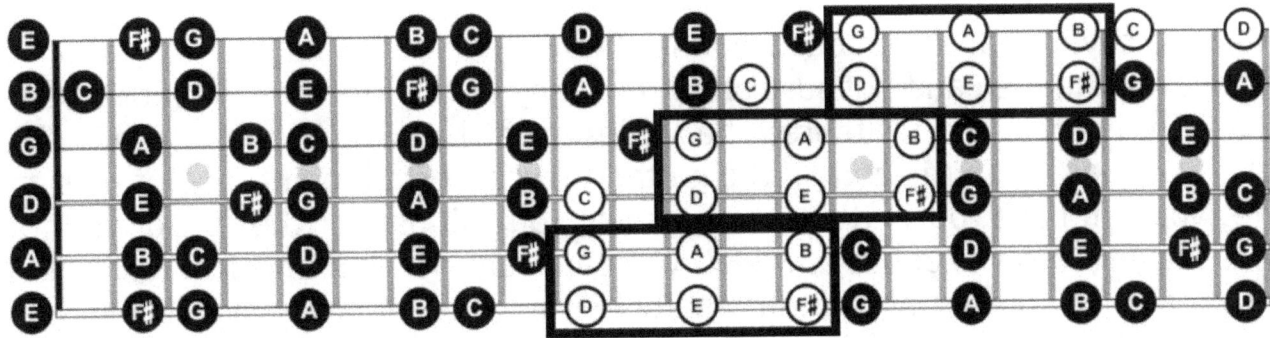

E AEOLIAN

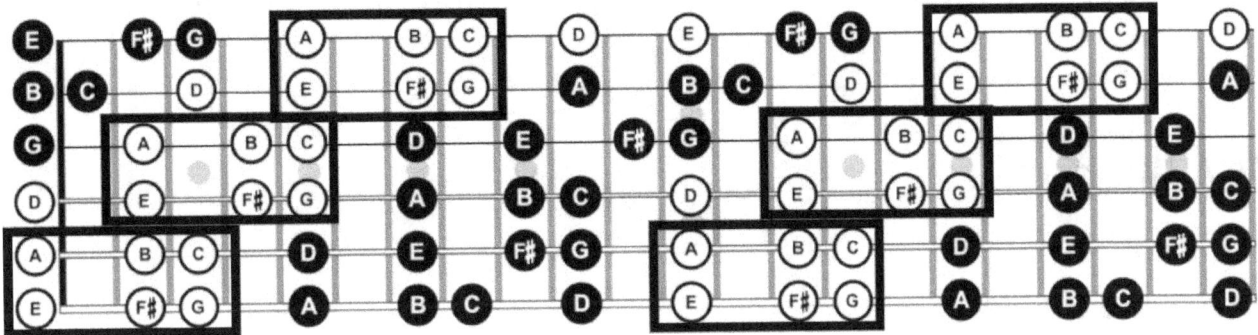

- You can really see the Neck Anatomy "shine" in E Aeolian.

- **REMEMBER these diagrams are only showing the Neck Anatomy from the E string, SHORT to LONG Octave** (Not showing the Short to Long octave from the A string).

- **In any mode ALL of its seven notes cover the entire fretboard.**

- I think of the box as 2 SHELL shapes followed by a FIRST FINGER SHIFT into the next octave.

- When you are moving octaves, pick up your hand as a unit so when you put it down in the new octave it is ready for all of the notes. Don't "inch worm."

- Neck Anatomy requires you to open your peripheral vision. You can use this "box" to visualize any mode moving across the fretboard in octaves.

- Remember, all of Neck Anatomy is sitting right on top of the same 5 patterns we have looked at.

REVIEW

We have covered an enormous amount of material and it's natural to feel a little overwhelmed and not sure about how any of this fits into the music you listen to. It does, and it's there. The Modes might be some of the last "new" stuff you learn in music and on the guitar. After a certain point in your musical life, you will have touched upon everything you will use for the rest of your life. Playing music is about how well you can translate your musical learnings into real time. It's not about continually learning brand new things. It's about using what you know, and using it to make people move and feel.

Learning music is a circular process and not a linear one.

As A Musician:

Modes as Melodies

When you open your mouth and sing a note, and then another and another, you are using the notes of a scale. That scale is a built with whole-steps and half-steps in different combinations. Each combination sounds different and these are modes. They are often iterations of the Major scale (Ionian) but there are others as well, like Harmonic minor and Melodic minor. They too each have modes, the same number of modes as notes.

Our Major scale is Ionian. If you tonicize the second note (play a melody so that the second note of that scale sounds like the ROOT) then you have a Dorian scale. We learned there are seven modes in the Major keys and they include three types of Major modes, three minor modes and one diminished.

Each mode, as a melody, has a unique sound. Ionian is ,"THE" Major, straight down the middle of the road vanilla sound. Dorian is the happy minor and Phrygian is the dark minor. Lydian is the exotic Major while Mixolydian is the funky Major. Aeolian is "THE" minor; serious, solemn and epic.

Modes as Chord Progression

Even without a melody, chords create modes too. Once we realize that any note in a Major scale can be the "main" note we can also see any of the chords in the key can be the "main" chord. This results in seven different modes, one for each chord. They have the same name and sound as the modes based on notes.

Every song is from some key and in some mode. Sometimes chords come from other keys and songs can change keys, but at some point you can see what key you are in. Music is predictable and learnable. The more songs you learn and study, the more you will see the same patterns.

The modes keep their mood and color despite whether it's melody, harmony or both that are creating the mode. If it's Dorian it will sound like Dorian, upbeat but minor, makes you crack a smile kind of minor. Dorian melodies do this and so do Dorian chord progressions.

The only thing that is always true is that the mode would be the same in the melody and chords. If you have a Dorian melody then the chords would have to be Dorian as well, and vice versa. If you have a Dorian chord progression then your melody will sound like Dorian. It is not possible to have a Dorian chord progression and a Mixolydian melody for example. The chords will always take precedent in the listeners ears as to what the "main" sound is. Meaning, if you are strumming a G chord, there is no way a listener will "hear" an A Dorian melody. It will sound like your playing a G Ionian scale starting on the second note, putting the wrong em-*phas*-is on the wrong sy-*lla*-ble.

As a Guitar Player:

We simply took our five patterns of pentatonics for the key of G and added two notes to our scale. These two notes created half-steps in each pentatonic pattern where there used to be a step and half gap in the scale.

I like to keep it simple. I just number the patterns, just like they were in the pentatonic. Remember the patterns are only there because most guitar players don't know the notes in their head or on the fretboard. Once you know both, patterns dissolve. You only need to fill in the five pentatonics to get all of the mode notes. It is totally unnecessary to think that there are seven physical patterns because there are seven notes.

PRACTICE

As a Musician

You have to develop this habit as a musician. **Look at every song with regard to the the Key and the Diatonic formula. Chord, key, mode.** Always look for it in EVERY song you ever play for the rest of your life. This is a process of elimination. Any one chord is only in three keys. From there you figure out the second chord, and usually by the third chord you will know what key and mode you are in.

Analyze songs, label the key and mode. Turn the progression into numbers, into it's relationship. You can then transpose it, and use it in other songs. It will help you remember music, figure out music and create music.

Always play music, instead of "practicing." Self generating is one of the simplest and most effective ways to do this aside from playing whole songs.

As A Guitar player

Once you know the Key and Mode you take pattern #1 to the fretboard, and think Rock and Roll Rule to get it in the right key. Now the other patterns are relative to it. Look for the ROOT note of the mode with Neck Anatomy.

Get to know Pattern #1 really well. Get to know it in all 12 keys. Remind yourself of the relative Major and minor from the "Rock and Roll Rule," as it applies to pattern #1.

You will always know that pattern #2 is above and pattern #5 is always behind pattern #1, flanking it. The other patterns just help move the sound of pattern #1's modes across your entire fretboard.

Drill the patterns, as quarter-notes, eighth-notes, triplets and sixteenth-notes. Sequence the patterns with three and four notes and more.

Start to look at the scales on one string and connect the patters vertically and horizontally. Eventually you want to see the whole fretboard light up with whatever key and mode you are in, and as a guitar player be able to get in and out of any notes any where on your instrument whenever you need to.

CHANGING KEYS AND MODES

Once you get comfortable with the Key of G it's time to try to move around to other keys. I found that getting the Key of G down was very helpful in relating to other keys and moving stuff around. The Key of A was an easy key to go to from G as everything is just two frets higher.

Get to know the keys you see and play in the most. There is an old school approach about always doing everything in all twelve keys, but that is a tall order. Quality over quantity. It is better to know a few keys very well than to half-ass all of them. You will have your whole life to get comfortable with all twelve keys.

Triads	I	ii	iii	IV	V	vi	vii dim
	I Major	ii minor	iii minor	IV Major	V Major	vi minor	vii dim
7th Chords	I Maj7	iim7	iiim7	IV Maj7	V7	vim7	vii-7b5
Modes	Ionian	Dorian	Phrygian	Lydian	Mixolydian	Aeolian	Locrian
DEGREE	TONIC	SUPER TONIC	MEDIANT	SUB DOMINANT	DOMINANT	SUB MEDIANT	LEADING TONE
SOUND	Relative MAJOR*	Happy minor	Dark+Heavy minor	Exotic Major	Funky Major	Relative MINOR*	dark and dim
KEYS 5ths ⬇	C	D	E	F	G	A	B
	G	A	B	C	D	E	F#
	D	E	F#	G	A	B	C#
	A	B	C#	D	E	F#	G#
	E	F#	G#	A	B	C#	D#
	B	C#	D#	E	F#	G#	A#
	Gb/F#	Ab/G#	Bb/A#	Cb/B	Db/C#	Eb/D#	F/E#
	Db	Eb	F	Gb	Ab	Bb	C
	Ab	Bb	C	Db	Eb	F	G
	Eb	F	G	Ab	Bb	C	D
	Bb	C	D	Eb	F	G	A
4ths ⬆	F	G	A	Bb	C	D	E

The following twelve pages have all the mode patterns for all the keys. They follow the Circle of Fifths.

Pick a key, name all of the notes, chords and modes. Navigate the five patterns for the key.

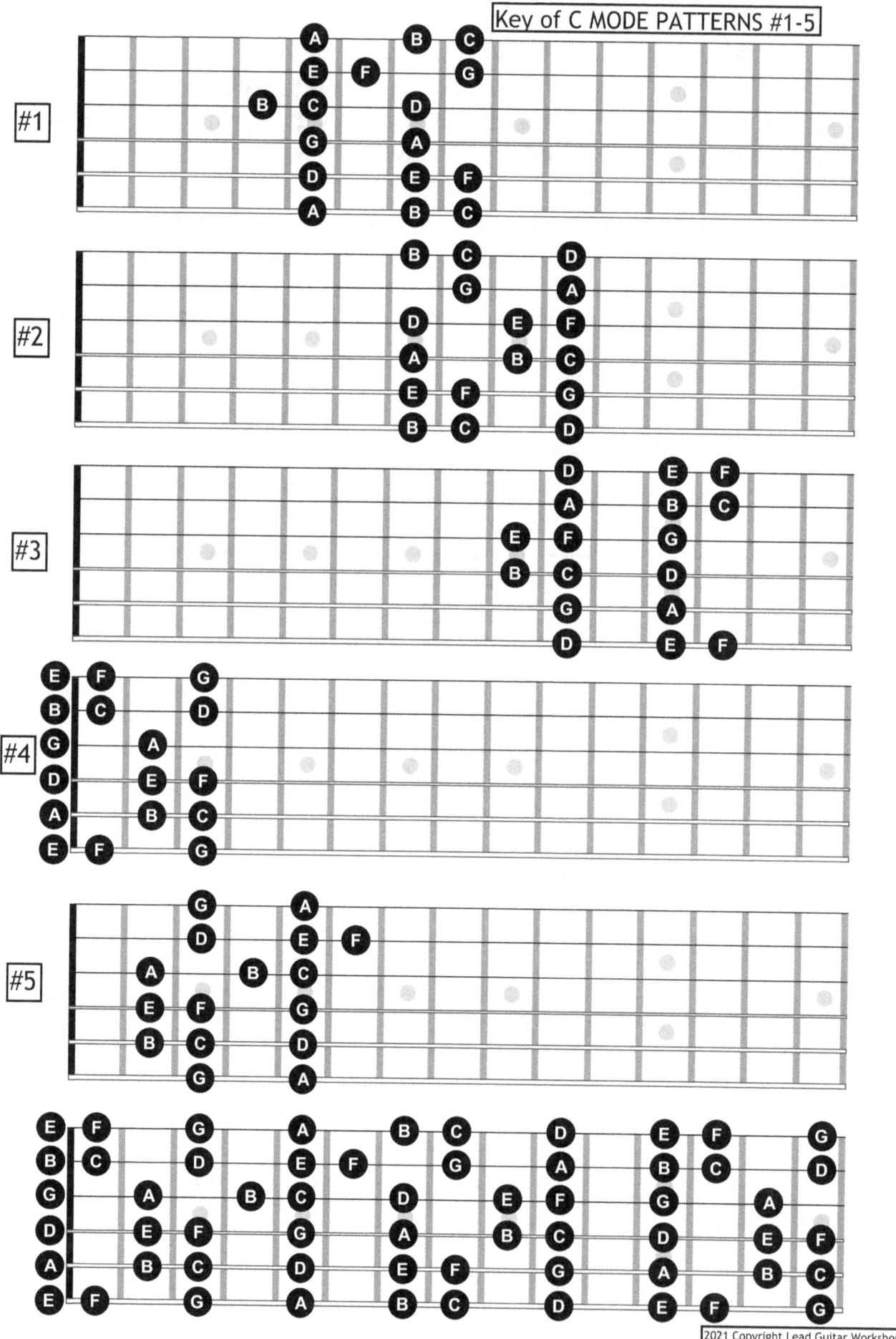

Key of C MODE PATTERNS #1-5

#1

#2

#3

#4

#5

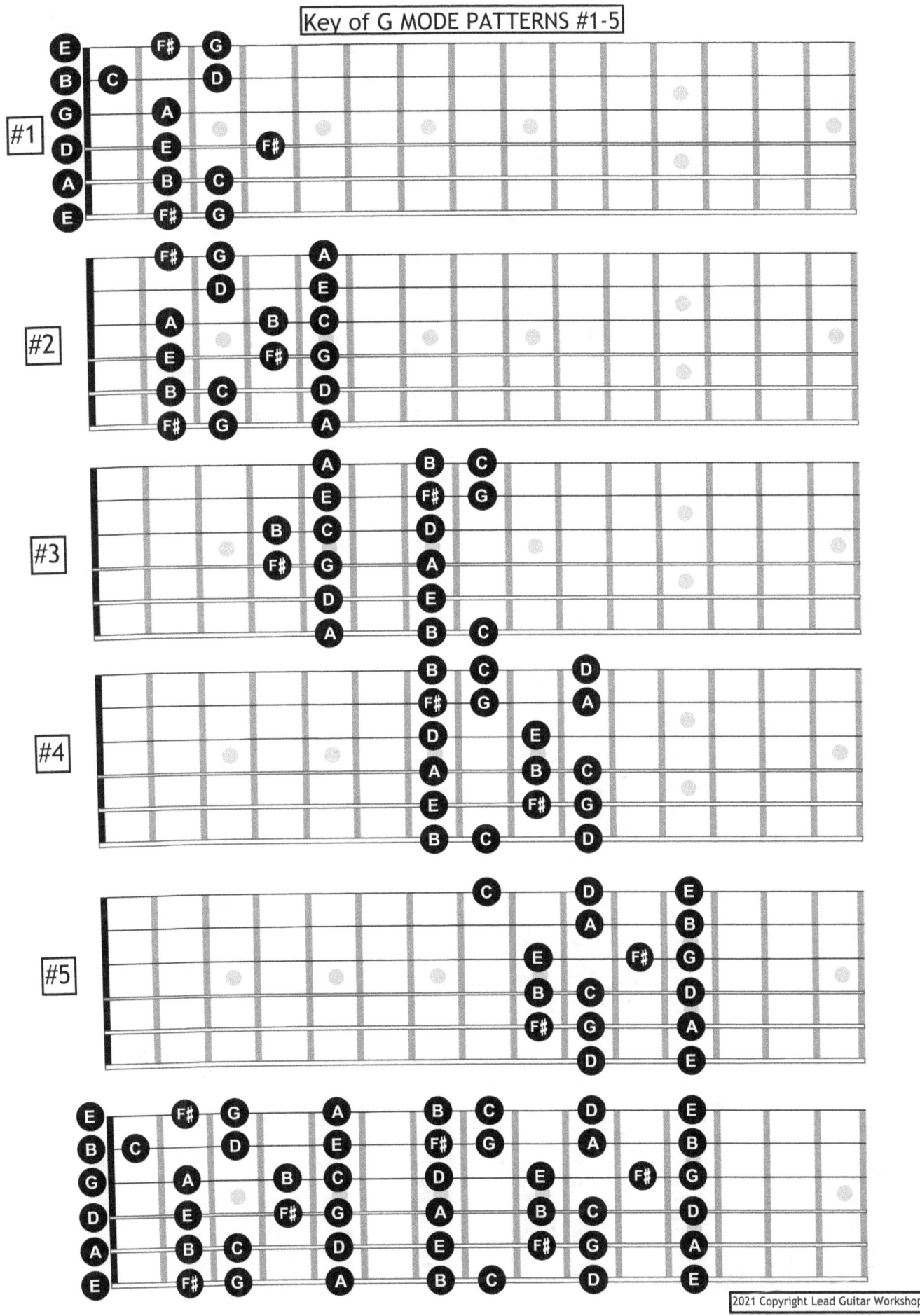

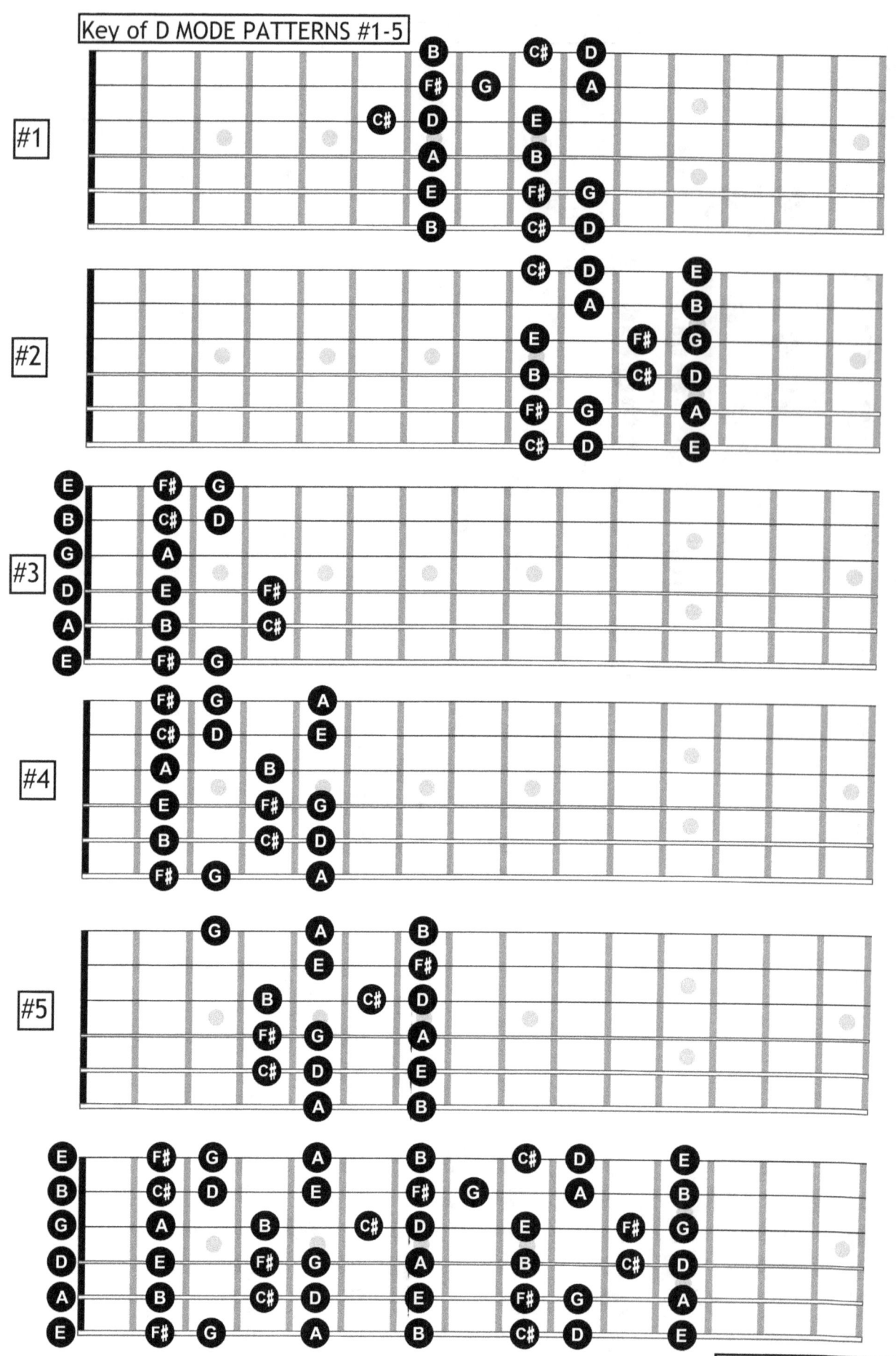

Key of D MODE PATTERNS #1-5

2021 Copyright Lead Guitar Workshop

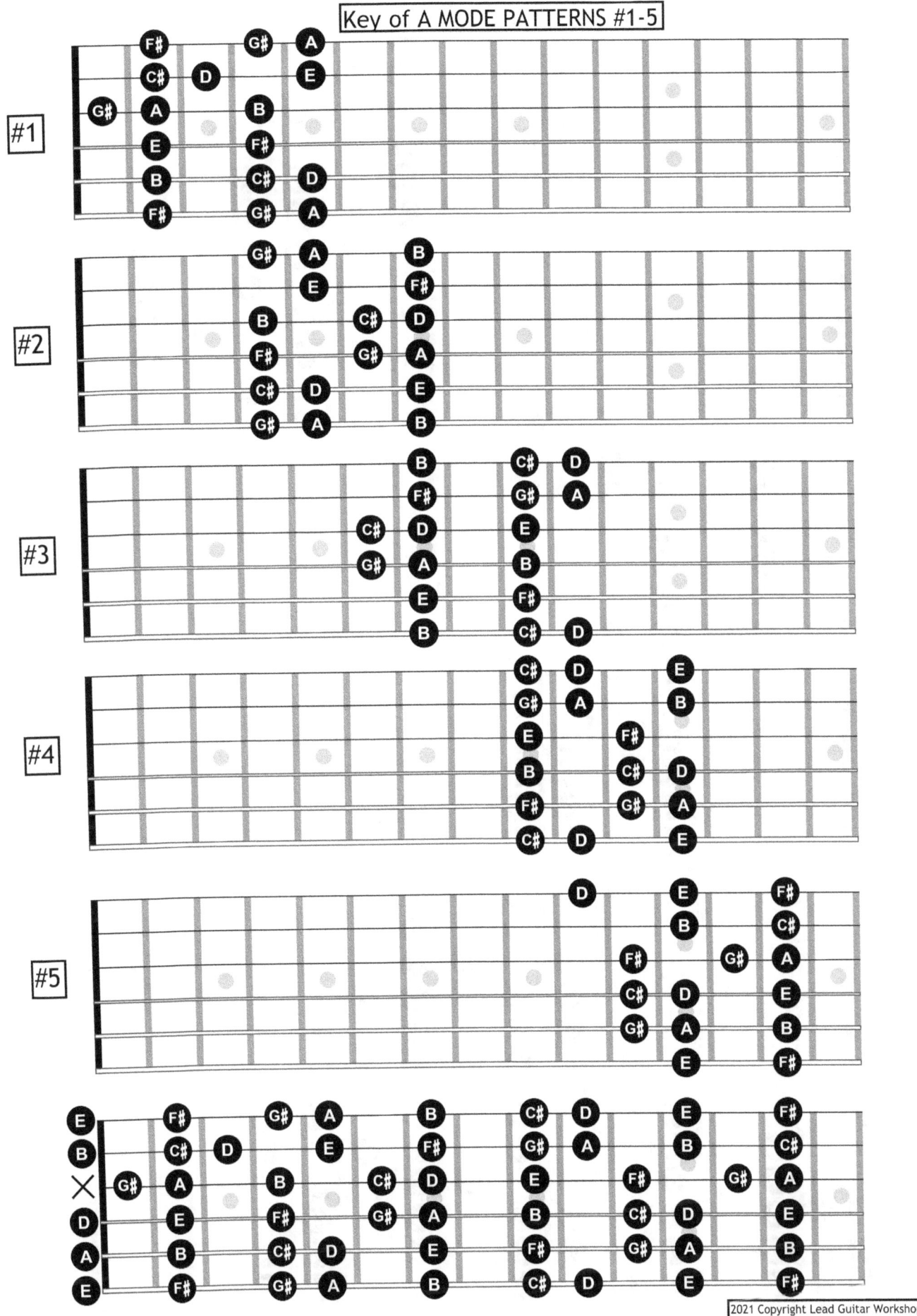

Key of A MODE PATTERNS #1-5

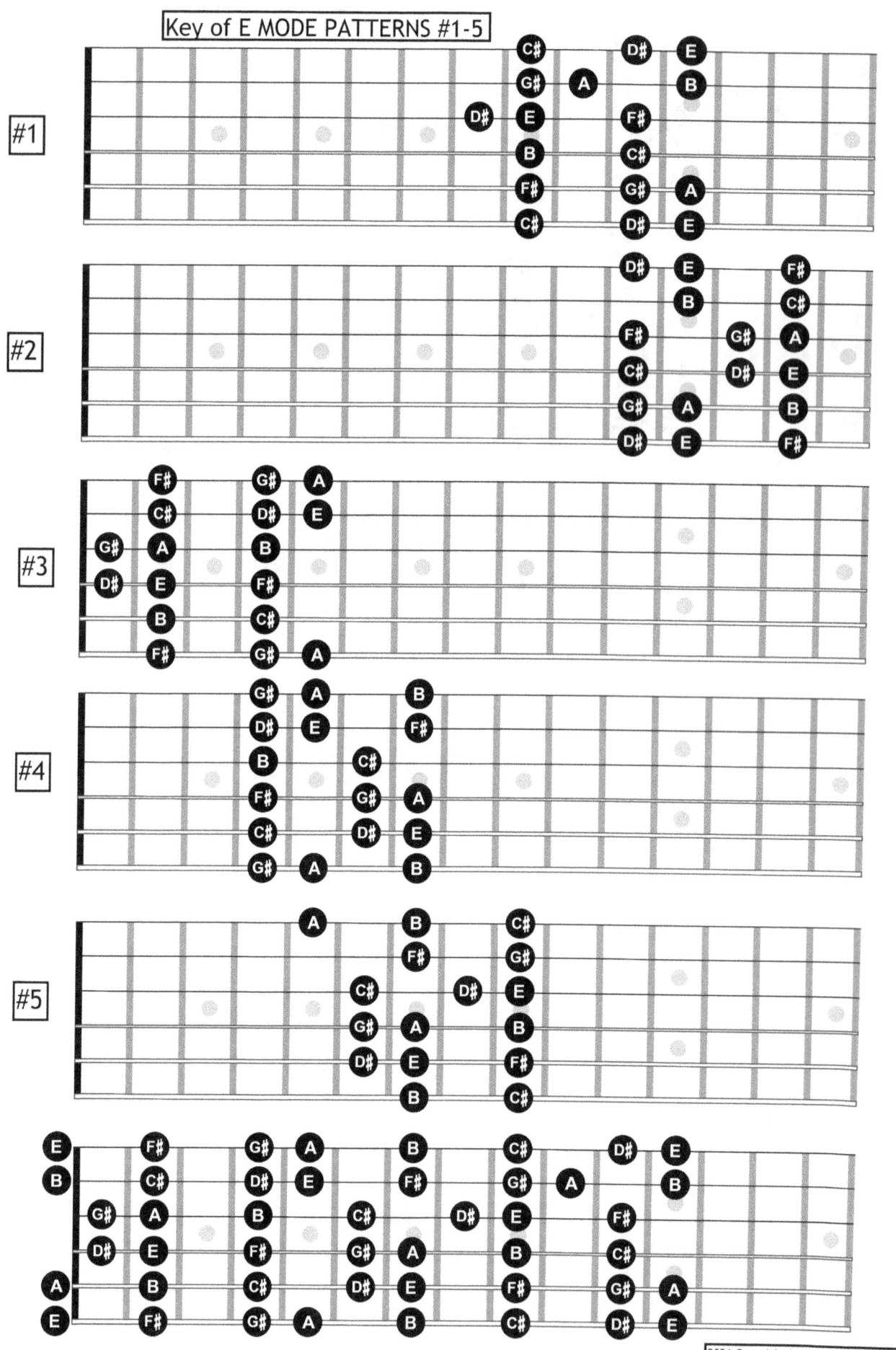

Key of E MODE PATTERNS #1-5

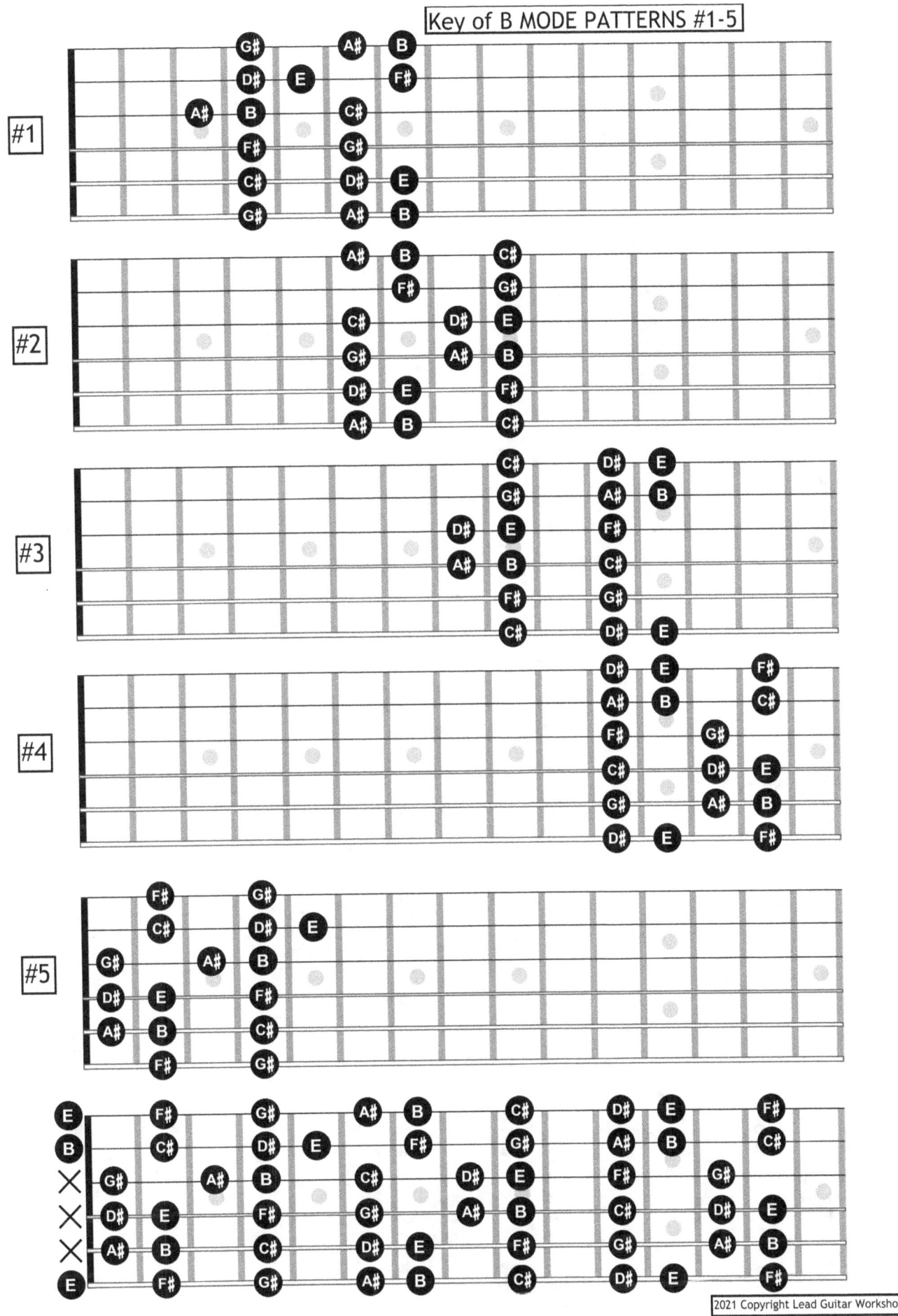

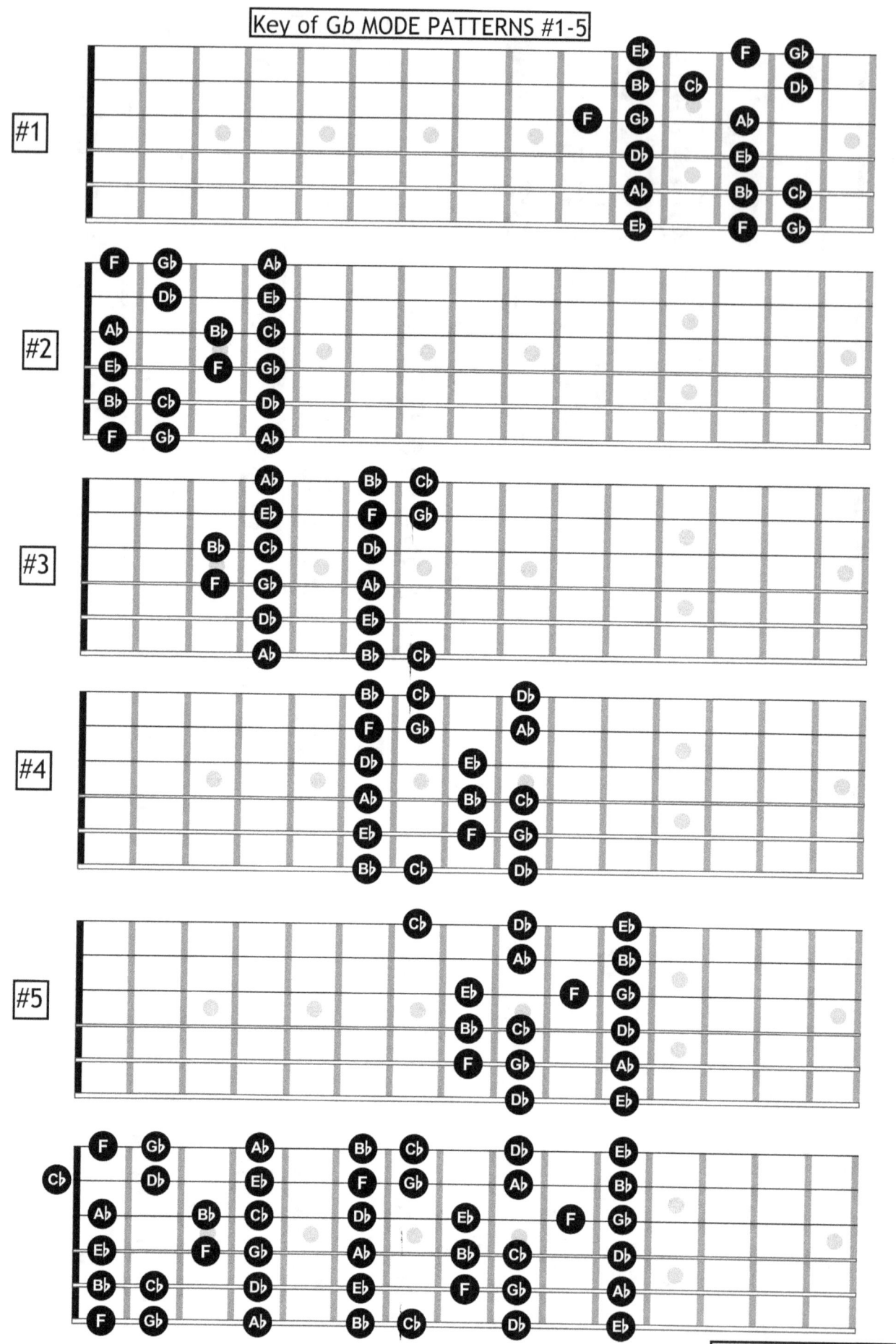

Key of G♭ MODE PATTERNS #1-5

2021 Copyright Lead Guitar Workshop

Key of D♭ MODE PATTERNS #1-5

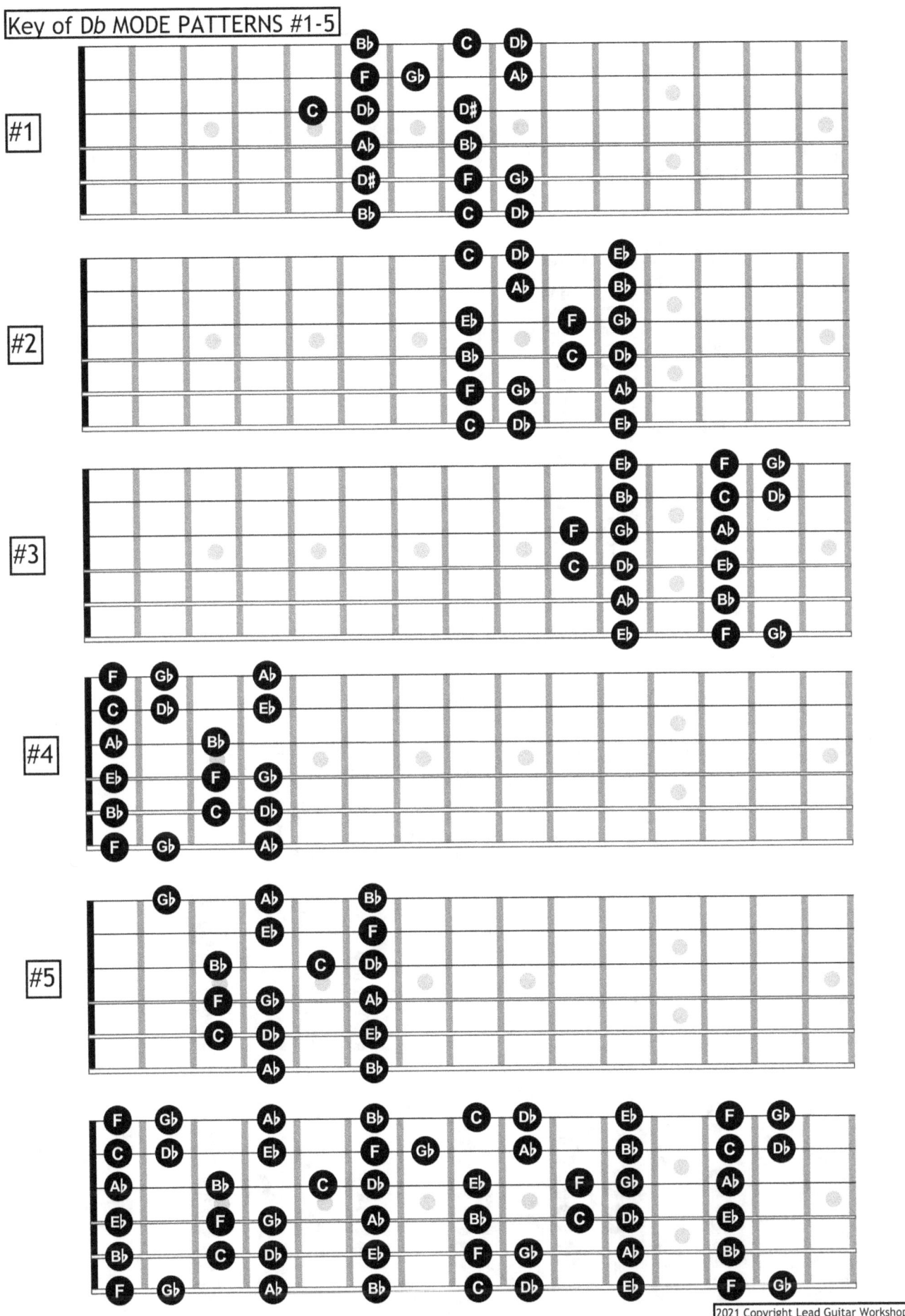

Key of A♭ MODE PATTERNS #1-5

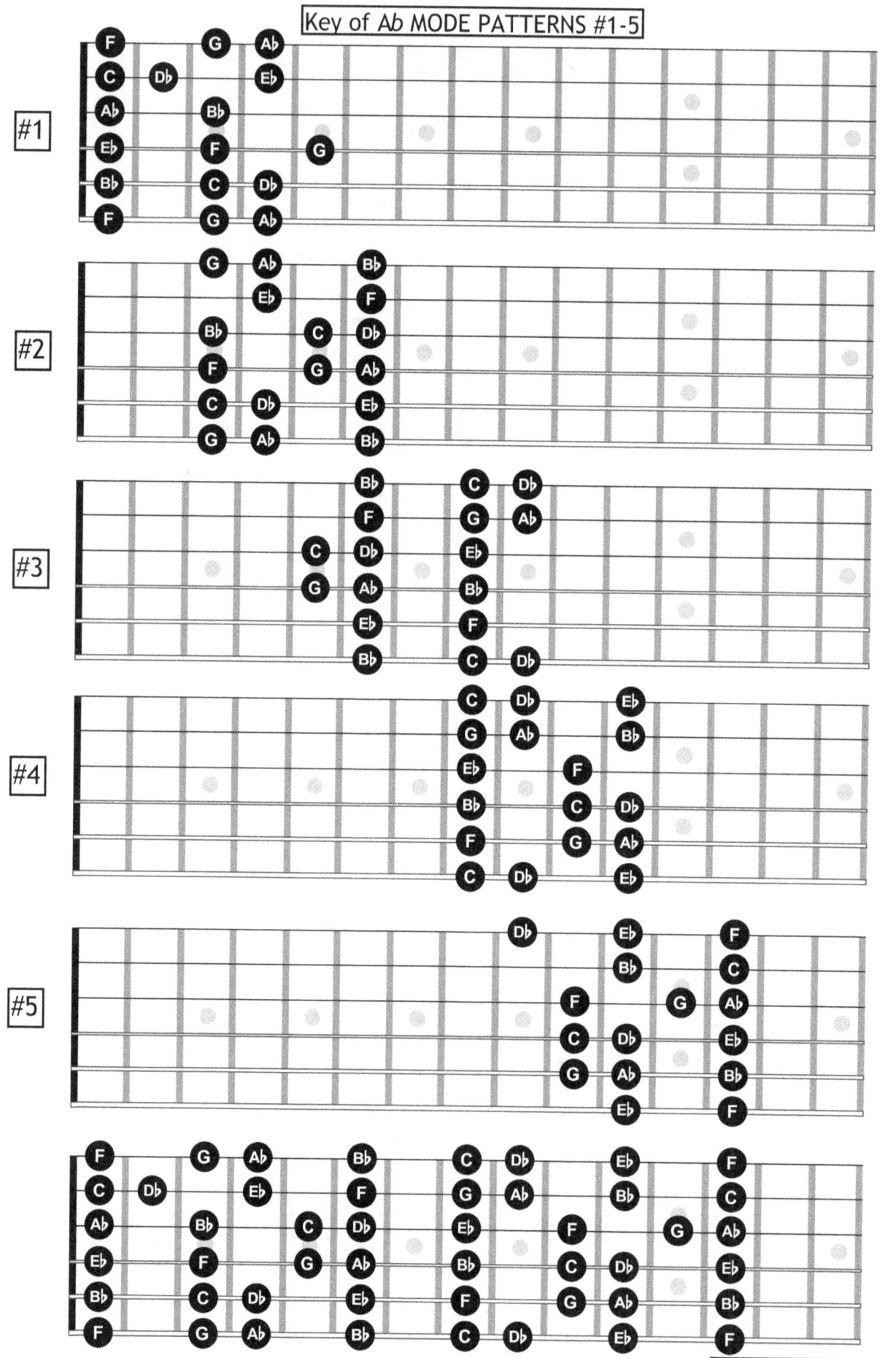

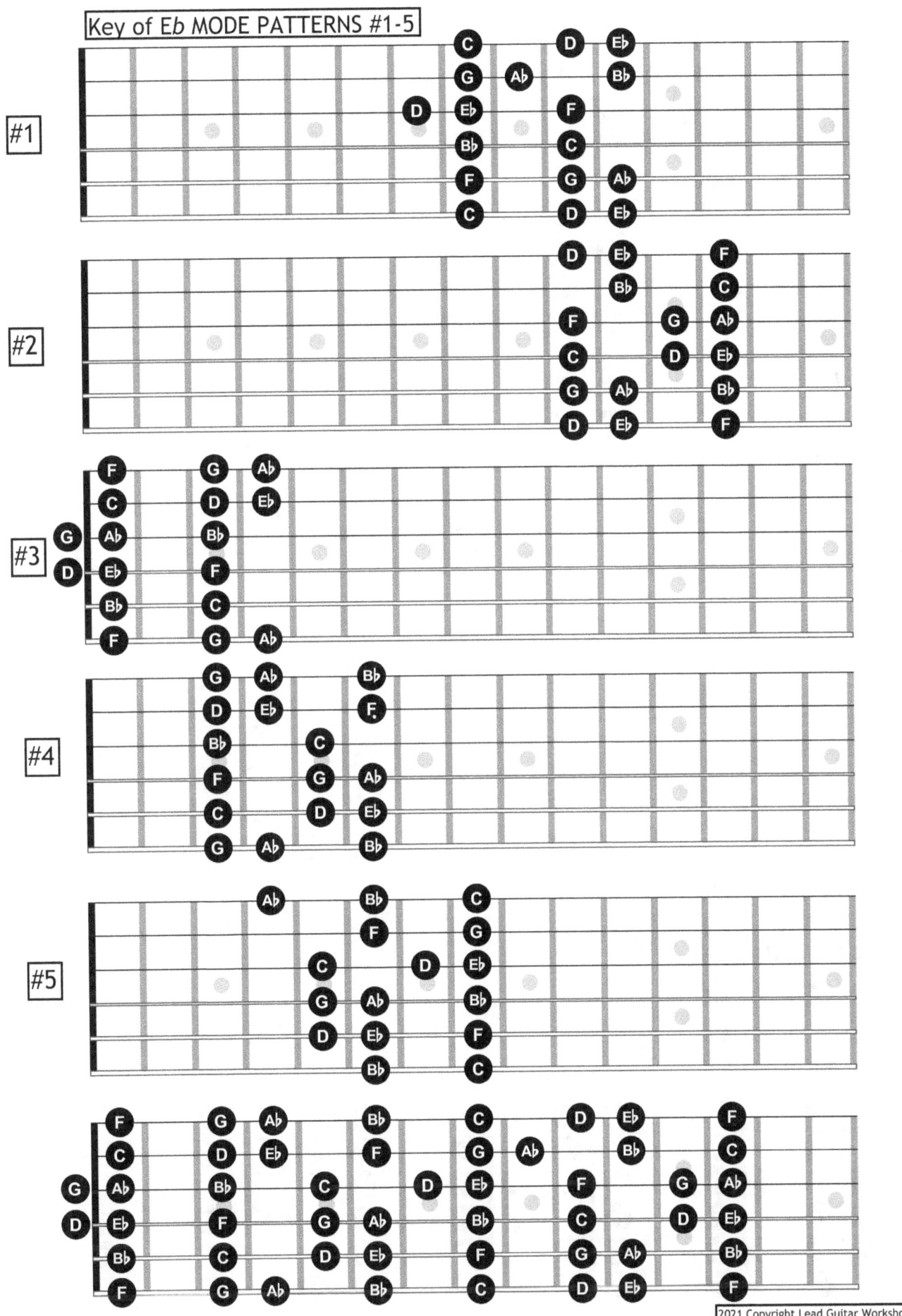

Key of Eb MODE PATTERNS #1-5

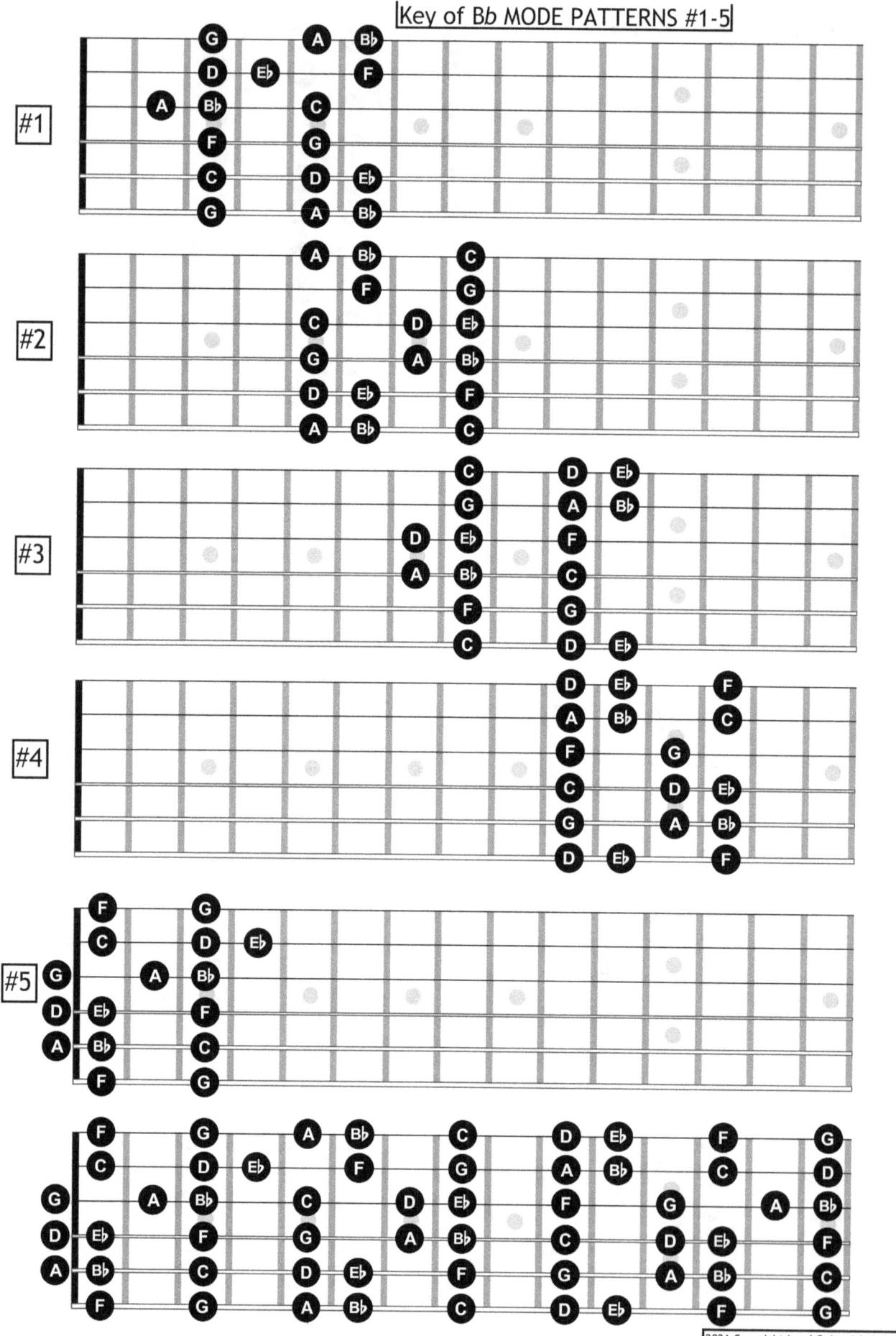

Key of B♭ MODE PATTERNS #1-5

2021 Copyright Lead Guitar Workshop

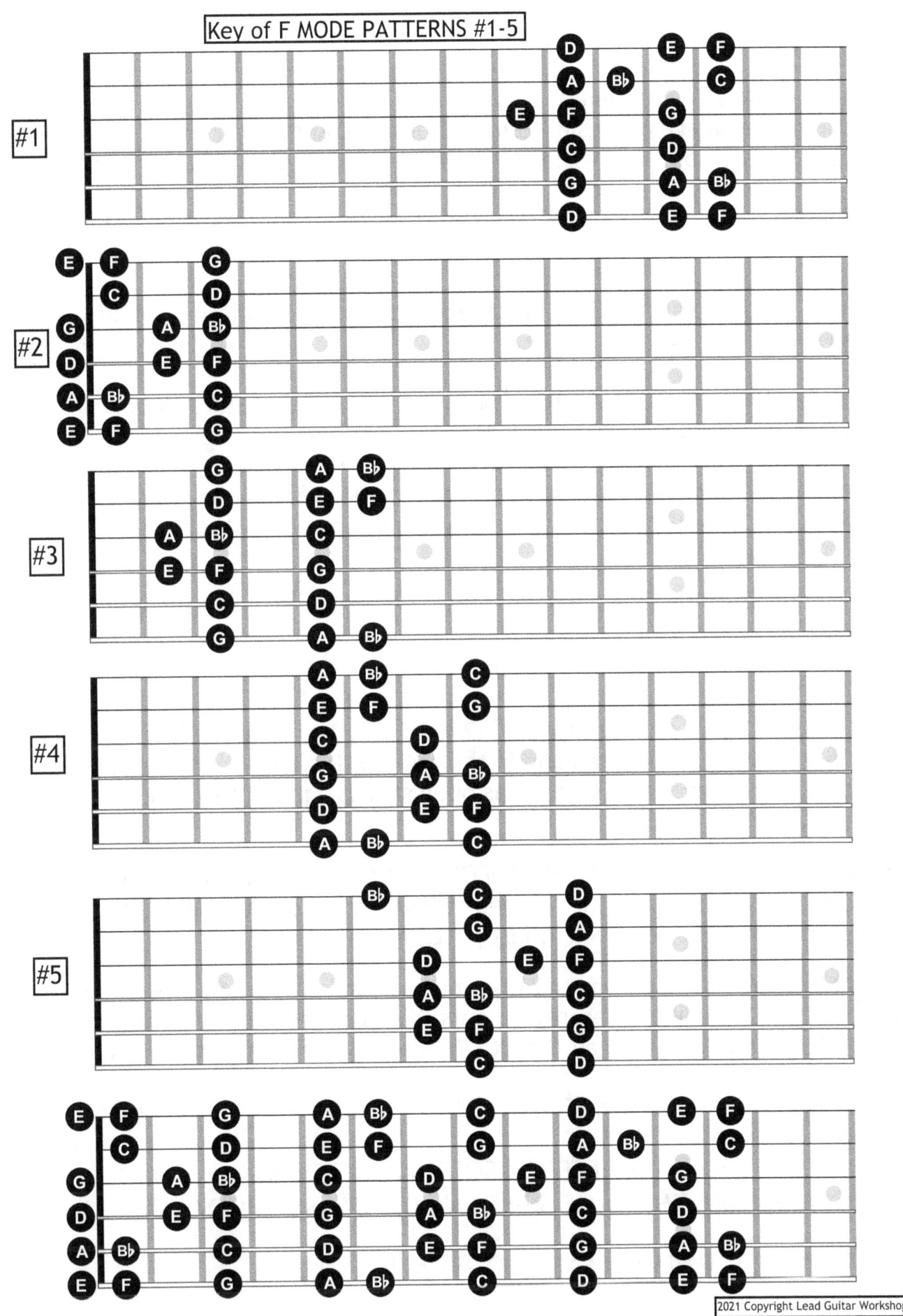

Key of F MODE PATTERNS #1-5

SUMMARY

We are musicians. We are guitar players.
We learn the language of music. Melody, Harmony, and Rhythm
We learn the craft of playing the guitar as an instrument.

MODES are a function of a SCALE. You can start any scale on any one of its own notes. This is melody.

The MODES are: **Ionian, Dorian, Phrygian, Lydian, Mixolydian, Aeolian, Locrian.**

MODES are CHORD PROGRESSIONS. You can use any of the chords in a key to be the "main" chord, the TONIC. This is Harmony.

We learn to see common modal chord progressions. We look for TRIADS and SEVENTH chords to help us determine Key, Mode, and when there are NON DIATONIC Chords.

Diatonic Harmony = I_{Maj7} ii_{m7} iii_{m7} IV_{Maj7} V_7 vi_{m7} vii_{m7b5}

As guitar players it is extremely helpful to see your octaves.

You will use ALL FIVE patterns for ALL 12 Keys, one key for each fret. The patterns are always connected and in the same order, always. Whatever goes past the 12th fret reappears starting as open strings again, like a giant conveyor belt.

We can use the ONE STRING MUSIC THEORY to help us see and hear the different intervals of the modes on one string. This also makes it easier to play on one string and not get stuck in just patterns.

NECK ANATOMY is the gateway to using your whole fretboard in a very musical and consistent way, like other instruments. You just need to memorize one (7) note pattern and move it to all the OCTAVES and play it in the same way.

We use BACKING TRACKS and SELF GENERATE to give a real time context to our playing.

ALL 5 PATTERNS SOUNDS THE SAME.
THEY ARE THE SAME SEVEN NOTES IN ANY GIVEN KEY.

HOW TO PRACTICE

Tune in - 5%
Take a few minutes to clear your head. Turn off your devices and do what you need before you dig in and play. Remind yourself that you are a musician and a guitar player. Everything you play should be rhythmically based, always.

Warm up - 10%
Muted String Ladders, Shells, and Changing Gears are some of the best warm ups. They simply get your fingers, hands, and internal clock all synchronized. Muted String ladders focus on rhythm and pick control. Changing Gears really harnesses the ability to feel and play rhythms. The Shells are best of both worlds and are like "wax on, wax off." Practice real world moves and patterns.

Exercise - 15%
This is where you run scales and patterns. This is a great opportunity to play through the five patterns. Always play them in time and play them ascending and descending or as "Round the Block" zigzag the patterns.

Review - 15%
Just as important as learning something new, make sure you're understanding something you have recently learned. It's essential to build your growth by reviewing past topics and understanding them deeper.

New Topic - 15%
Learn something new. However easy or small, it is growth. Every little bit moves you towards your goal of sounding great as a musician. Maybe it's learning the names of the notes in a scale, or a lick, a chord, anything that helps you sound better. You can learn as a musician, as a guitar player, and as a rhythmist.

"Practice" - 40%
The best way to practice is not to practice, but to play! It's true. Every one of our heroes played music more than anything else. Practicing refers to some future date that you are preparing for. Playing is now. Play in time, carry the song, the beat, the groove, all of it. Self-Generating is the best way to play and get your practicing in. If you are practicing a turnaround in a blues, then you play the 12 bar blues and at the end you play the turnaround. If you miss it, keep playing and get it the next time around. This is what you would do onstage. Keep playing and you will get better, as you would if you "practiced."

THOUGHTS

The learning path in music is circular. You will learn something and come back around to it and get to know it better. Every time you do this you will gain more confidence and experience. There is only so much actual information you will need to learn. It is all about how to use and manipulate that material that makes the magic of music start. Learning music is not a linear path but a circular one.

Music is Melody (notes), Harmony (chords), and Rhythm.
Rhythm is the number one factor to sounding great.

Where attention goes, energy flows. So much of being a better musician is all about your mind set and what you focus your time and energy on.

"The process of learning consists not in what is brought to the learner, but what is drawn out of him." (Plato)

"The Student as a boxer, not a fencer. The Fencer's weapon is picked up and put down again. The Boxer's is part of him, all he has to do is clench his fist." (Marcus Aurelius-Meditations)

"The Student as a musician, not a guitarist. The guitarist's instrument is picked up and put down. The musician's is part of him. All he has to do is tap, clap, and sing." (Suke Cerulo)

You can play music without melody (just chords) and you can play music without chords (just melody, like your voice), but you can *never* play music without rhythm, it's impossible. As soon as you tap your foot or pluck a note, rhythm happens.

The language of music hasn't really changed in hundreds of years. It is much older than the guitar. Once you know the language, that's it. Now you can learn as many instruments as you want. You just have to adapt to the physical part of the instrument.

The instrument is silent without you. You are music!

GLOSSARY

Audiation Inner Hearing but also the musical knowledge behind it, to hear the knowledge.

Arpeggio The notes of a chord played in succession rather than simultaneously.

BPM Beats-per-minute. How music tempo/beat/quarter-note is measured.

Chord Usually three or more notes played simultaneously.

Chord Inversion The notes of a chord rotating in order (example R35, 35R, 5R3).

Chord Scale The scale matched to a particular chord, using its chord tones and appropriate notes in between to best fit for playing the changes.

Chord Tone A single note, as part of a chord.

Degree, Scale The number in the scale at which a note lives. There are seven notes in the diatonic scale. They are numbered 1-7 for their degrees.

Diatonic meaning "of the key". Notes and chords only in that key.

Diatonic Harmony The seven chords that naturally occur in all keys and its resulting formula.   (I ii iii IV V vi viidim)

Fingerpicking/Fingerstyle Fingerpicking is using fingers only to pluck the strings on guitar. Fingerstyle might include thumb and/or fingerpicks.

Gear (LGW) Slang for describing the different rhythms. First gear is quarter-notes, second gear is eighth-notes; third gear is triplets; fourth gear is sixteenth-notes, and so on.

Half-step The smallest interval in music. It is one fret on a guitar, and a single piano key to the next (for example white to black)

<u>Harmonic Rhythm</u> The rhythmic pacing of chord changes; how often the chords change (for example every two beats versus every four beats).

<u>Harmony</u> Chords or notes being played simultaneously to produce a sonorous sound. Chord progressions and the underlying chord motion.

<u>HO PO</u> Short for Hammer-ons and Pull-offs

<u>Hybrid Picking</u> When you combine the use of a pick and the remaining three fingers to get a combination of flat pick and fingerstyle.

<u>Inner Hearing</u> Hearing music in your inner ear by memory even if you don't know it musically. (Happy Birthday, Hot Cross buns, and others)

<u>Key</u> One of 12 families built around the 7 note Major scale. Contains 7 chords, one for each of its own notes built by the Rule of Thirds.

<u>Legato</u> When a musician connects the notes of a phrase in a smooth and consistent sound without any silence in between the notes.

<u>Lick</u> A slang term used to describe a group of notes, usually used in a lead solo. These can be recognized by style, genre, person, and more.

<u>LGW</u> <u>Lead Guitar Workshop</u>

<u>Melody</u> One note-at-a-time succession of notes in a pleasing fashion. The signature of a song and the part that is copyright protected.

<u>Mode</u> A function of a scale/key. When a Key or scale is based on any one of its chords/notes. This changes the half-steps in relation to where they live in the scale, producing varying sounds of Major and minor chord progressions and scales.

<u>Monophonic</u> Producing one note-at-a-time only.

<u>Muted String Ladder</u> (MSL)(LGW) A picking hand exercise to improve rhythm and confidence in Down, Up, and Alternate picking across the strings

<u>Musical Truth</u> (LGW) A term to describe some of the fundamental rules in music that every musician follows regardless of instrument.

<u>Neck Anatomy</u> (LGW) Using octaves in a short to long connection to help navigate the fretboard and move around like other instruments do and not be tied to changing patterns. There are 2 pairs of "short to long" octaves (E and A string).

<u>Pentatonic</u> Meaning "five notes of the home." These are ancient five note scales believed to have originated in Asia. There are two main types, Major and minor, and they are in all types of music all around the planet.

<u>Playing the changes</u> A slang term a musician uses when they change their note choices/scales/arpeggios to match each individual chord instead of a "Global" sound of playing one scale for all the chords.

<u>Polyphonic</u> The ability to play multiple notes simultaneously. Pianos and guitars are polyphonic, the human voice is not.

<u>Riff</u> A slang term for rhythm guitar part made up of notes instead of chords. Think "Heartbreaker" by Led Zeppelin, "Crazy Train" by Ozzy.

<u>Rhythm</u> The pulse in music. The basis for everything music. The measured beat and its subdivisions.

<u>Root</u> The "main" note in a Key/chord/scale/arpeggio. The one everything else revolves around. The sound that comes home resolves to the Root.

<u>Root Position</u> When a scale pattern, arpeggio, or chord shape has its ROOT as the lowest note.

<u>Rule of Thirds</u> Stacking every other note in a scale to create a chord. Three notes for a triad and four notes for a seventh chord.

<u>Self-Gen</u> (LGW) Using your inner ear and inner clock to start and play music yourself, in time, especially with consideration of switching between chords and soloing.

<u>Shell</u> (LGW) A hand dexterity exercise to help overcome any guitar playing issue. It involves a fingering, a performance method, and rhythm.

Staccato Each note is sharply detached or separated from the others.

Tied In music notation when an arch connects two or more rhythms to create a sustained sound. Especially useful to achieve lengths of time not possible with traditional rhythms (for example a note that last 1 ½ quarter notes.)

Tonic The "main" note/chord. Often the key but not always. It is the note/chord that everything else resolves to.

Tresillo A Latin based rhythmic figure where 8 eighth-notes are grouped in 3 3 2 notes to total 8.

Triad A three note chord. Usually achieved by stacking every other note in a scale for a total of three notes.

Voice Leading A term used for connecting the chord tones of one chord to another with the notes moving the least amount necessary to make the chord change. This makes a really smooth sound.

Whole-step The second smallest interval in music. It is two half-steps in distance. Most scales consist of half-steps and whole-steps.

ABOUT AUTHOR

Michael Cerulo (aka Suke) is a guitarist and multi-instrumentalist whose life long love and devotion to music has given him a very distinct and identifiable sound. Whether it's his fluid guitar melodies, the warm organic tone of his flute, or his own recordings where he plays and produces all of the music, Suke's individuality, creativity and talent are evident in all of his creations.

Born in a suburb of Boston, Suke was raised in a musical family. His grandfather (George Lane) was a composer, multi-instrumentalist and bandleader during the late 40's and early 50's. All four of George's siblings were musicians as well, often being employed in his big band. The youngest brother helped start **Berklee College of Music**. Suke began playing guitar and taking music lessons when he was twelve. Being persistent, with an unbending intent to learn and grow, he then enrolled in Berklee College of Music in Boston. After graduating in '94, while also working for MOTU music software, Suke became a full time touring musician. Suke composed, played guitar and flute with his band **Schleigho**.

Schleigho (pronounced shlay-ho) was formed at Berklee in 1993 and was touring around the country a year later. The band's style is a mix of jazz and funk, with each of its four members contributing equally to bring about an unprecedented wall of sound. Being predominately instrumental, the band's incredible talent and versatility allows them to go from opening for the Allman Brothers to playing high scale jazz venues while satisfying the most discriminating of tastes. The band released their first CD (*self-titled*) in 1995, '*Farewell to the Sun*' in 1997 and '*In the Interest of Time*' in 1998. In 2000 the band signed with **Flying Frog Records (owned and managed by members of the Allman Brothers)**. Under Flying Frog Records they released '*Continent*' in 2000, and '*Live at HoDown 2000*' the following year. Schleigho has met with great success over the years; from amassing a substantial and dedicated national following to '*Continent*' breaking into the top 20 on CMJ and college Jazz radio charts. Averaging over 200 shows annually across the country, they have shared the stage with **The Allman Brothers band, Derek Trucks, Bela Fleck, John Scofield, Karl Denson, Maceo Parker, G. Love and Special Sauce, Galactic, moe. and Soulive**, to name a few. Schleigho has performed at the JVC Jazz festival (NYC), the Gathering of the Vibes, the High Sierra Music Festival, and the Berkshire Music Festival, among others, and are veterans of the club/college circuit and large festival scene for over 20 years.

Suke also performed for years with the band **Conehead Buddha**, which is a song structured improvisational fusion of hip-hop, rock, and jazz, flirting with many styles from drum and bass to latin and reggae. It's a high energy show featuring Terence and Shannon Lynch.

Another avenue he has been steadily involved with is the production of music for multimedia. For the last twenty years Suke has been developing his production and engineering abilities in his own project studio to further enhance his musical visions. He created *Tone Over Tone* in which he composes, performs, engineers, mix's and masters recordings to be licensed for multimedia applications. This area of music production allows for infinite amounts of creation and timbre. Using conventional instruments, modern technology and a thorough musical background, Suke now creates breathtaking music that utilizes almost any instrument in creation with lush sound design.

His sound is refreshing and his performance is intense. You can always hear diverse musical influences throughout his compositions and soloing. Music from the likes of Jimi Hendrix and Van Halen to John Coltrane, Roland Kirk, and George Benson. From Jeff Beck and Ozzy to Herbie Hancock, Mingus and Miles. From Igor Stravinsky to Square Pusher and Amon Tobin.

Suke currently resides in New York City with his family and has been the *Director of Lead Guitar Program at New York City's "Best" Guitar School* since 2004. He has taught over 15,000 lessons and classes amassing a staggering amount of teaching experience. Suke is also responsible for the musical evaluations of incoming teachers and has often taught the other teachers at the school. The hundreds of students and thousands of hours teaching have help sculpt and mold the success of his teaching methods.

Whether it's playing in a group context, performing, teaching or creating and producing music, Suke always incorporates a fine balance of taste and technique with a result that's not soon forgotten. He always keeps his eye and ear to the future while respectfully paying homage to his influences and tradition.